Cigarettes & Wine

Social Fictions Series

Series Editor
Patricia Leavy
USA

The *Social Fictions* series emerges out of the arts-based research movement. The series includes full-length fiction books that are informed by social research but written in a literary/artistic form (novels, plays, and short story collections). Believing there is much to learn through fiction, the series only includes works written entirely in the literary medium adapted. Each book includes an academic introduction that explains the research and teaching that informs the book as well as how the book can be used in college courses. The books are underscored with social science or other scholarly perspectives and intended to be relevant to the lives of college students—to tap into important issues in the unique ways that artistic or literary forms can.

Please email queries to pleavy7@aol.com

Cigarettes & Wine

J. E. Sumerau

SENSE PUBLISHERS
ROTTERDAM/BOSTON/TAIPEI

A C.I.P. record for this book is available from the Library of Congress.

ISBN: 978-94-6300-927-0 (paperback)
ISBN: 978-94-6300-928-7 (hardback)
ISBN: 978-94-6300-929-4 (e-book)

Published by: Sense Publishers,
P.O. Box 21858,
3001 AW Rotterdam,
The Netherlands
https://www.sensepublishers.com/

All chapters in this book have undergone peer review.

Printed on acid-free paper

ADVANCE PRAISE FOR
CIGARETTES & WINE

"With same-sex marriage rights having been ruled constitutional, people who differ from the binary gender norm are finding new ways to communicate the countless ways in which reality challenges simplistic gender stereotypes. To some observers, this seems a nightmare of terrifying disorder. To others, it is a moment for true, even sacred, liberation. Still others won't know what to make of it at all. This small-town coming-of-age novel might help people anywhere along this spectrum to understand what it is like to live where navigating others' conceptions of masculinity and femininity is at once a necessary survival skill and an obstacle to self-understanding. In fact, I suspect that many people who have even unrecognized ambivalences about sexual and gender binaries might find in it an illuminating reflection of their own paths. This fast-paced, introspective romp through high school and beyond keeps the pages turning with love, sex, and an understanding grandma."
– Dawne Moon, Ph.D., Marquette University and author of *God, Sex, and Politics: Homosexuality and Everyday Theologies*

"Weeks after reading *Cigarettes & Wine*, I'm still having a hard time believing it is a work of fiction. The characters feel so real in their emotions, interactions, complexities, and flaws that I assumed the author had simply done a good job of recounting experiences from zir own life. The characters are people I would want to know in real life, their experiences are the kind I would become engrossed in as a friend. When I finished the book, I was disappointed that my time as an observer in their lives had come to an end. *Cigarettes & Wine* is entertaining, thrilling, heartbreaking, while also a bit educational about the often invisible members of the LGBTQ community – bi and pan sexual, trans and gender non-conforming, and polyamorous folks. You won't want to put it down!"
– Eric Anthony Grollman, Ph.D., University of Richmond and Editor of ConditionallyAccepted.com

"J Sumerau's novel is a funny, painful, powerful exploration of identity in the rural American South. Grounded both in Sumerau's personal experience and zir extensive research in gender, religion, and sexualities, the novel depicts the complex processes involved in existing and connecting with others in social settings that are at once hidden and highly visible, and in which the risk of exposure of multiple kinds creates an ever-present structural force that shapes the narrator's developing identity. Written from a first-person perspective that allows the reader to envision zirself in the narrator's shoes, *Cigarettes & Wine* provides a fantastic teaching tool, addressing myriad issues related to inequalities and identities."
– Brandy Simula, Ph.D., Emory University

"*Cigarettes & Wine* offers a humanizing look into an adolescent's journey through desire, love, and discovering their place in the world. A bold and brave contribution to the discipline, *Cigarettes & Wine* is an exemplary model for coupling storytelling and Sociology. A captivating read for all those studying gender and sexuality and for anyone interested in a coming of age narrative of a gender and sexually nonconforming individual navigating a heteronormative world. Much praise to J Sumerau for what can best be described as a one-of-a-kind narrative of pain and passion."
– Katie Acosta, Ph.D., Georgia State University

"This wonderful novel uplifts as it challenges us to consider the invisible lives of queer and bisexual working class teens living and loving in the Evangelical South of the 1990s. Nostalgic, joyous, painful, and raw, *Cigarettes & Wine* strips away the shiny veneer of the coming-of-age novel and delivers powerful lessons about sexuality, gender, class, and youth. Sumerau's characters inspire, reminding us of the best that can exist in people even in the worst of circumstances. *Cigarettes & Wine* is a valuable contribution to social science fiction, which may prove invaluable in classes focused on gender, sexualities, class, and the ways our social experiences influence the people we become."
– Katherine McCabe, MA, Doctoral Candidate and Instructor, University of Illinois Chicago

"In my classes, I seek to emotionally engage students with the powerful ways of knowing sociology offers for everyday life, reflexivity, and social change. Unfortunately, standard textbooks typically fall entirely short in this regard, and often leave many marginalized communities and experiences unrepresented. On the other hand, *Cigarettes & Wine* is an exceptional example of how evocative, captivating, accessible, and inclusive storytelling can and should be used to promote sociological lessons for students far beyond classrooms. It is quite difficult to think of a course where I would not incorporate this work as it speaks to so many topics of great importance to sociologists – gender, sexualities, religion, relationships, families, and emotion to name just a few. What I find most appealing is its raw and unapologetic honesty, as well as its unique privileging of complexity. Sumerau makes no use of 'sunshine' or 'smoke,' but instead constructs a 'show-don't-tell' exhibition of the type of confusion and sense-making, love and loss, pain and endurance, life and death, support and abdication that may accompany 'being' and 'becoming' Queer youth in our society."
– **Maggie Cobb, Ph.D., University of Tampa**

"*Cigarettes & Wine* is not just a marvelously written coming of age story, it is the bisexual, transgender coming of age story we so desperately need today. I cried my eyes out, laughed until my abdomen was sore, and felt connected to these characters in a way that transcends time and space. Be ready to feel the wind through your hair on the ride to the lake, the cool Carolina grass between your toes while walking through the park, and the very real pain of loss mixed with the joy of teenage discovery. As a bisexual, genderqueer scholar, *Cigarettes & Wine* feels like a fictional ethnography because I know these people, I've adventured with them, and had to say tearful goodbyes to a few of them along the way. An emotional rollercoaster, *Cigarettes & Wine* is a journey I recommend to any reader interested in Queer coming of age stories."
– **Lain A.B. Mathers, M.A., Doctoral Candidate and Instructor, Univerity of Illinois Chicago**

"Narrative is pedagogically timeless. A tool that allows strangers to relate by getting to know characters and context, stories help make abstract, academic concepts concrete. In *Cigarettes & Wine*, Sumerau enables anyone to step into the character's shoes to better understand life, context, and coming of age in a society that labels non-mainstream beliefs, behaviors, and identities shameful or wrong. With humor and emotional candor, this story allows the reader to follow along with the challenges of growing up while trying to become the most authentic version of oneself, while also helping readers unfamiliar with scholarly approaches to gender and sexuality ascertain ideas on a human scale that they may have only read about in a detached way on the internet. Readers can't help but empathize with the common struggles and desires for recognition and acceptance which are universal to us all. I believe this book is a useful addition for teachers or seekers alike who wish to expand their horizons beyond the constrained categorizations embedded in society to the larger multifaceted and nonconforming liminal hues of humanity."
– Sarrah Conn, Ph.D., Hillsborough Community College

"*Cigarettes & Wine* is an unflinching account of coming into one's gender and sexuality at the intersection of curiosity, pleasure and religion. It is an honest take on the ways we relate to others, sexually and emotionally, that would benefit students across disciplines like Women's Studies, Sexuality Studies and Sociology. By reading *Cigarettes & Wine*, marginalized students would get an important opportunity to see themselves in text and others a chance to learn about bisexual and non-binary people that mainstream LGBTQ efforts refuse to prioritize in media and scholarship."
– Simone Kolysh, M.A., M.P.H., Doctoral Candidate and Instructor, City University of New York

To those who embody sexual and gender fluidity in a world that seeks to erase us, and especially to Xan for continuously inspiring me to do the same even when it hurts

TABLE OF CONTENTS

PREFACE

Imagine the terror and exhilaration of a first sexual experience in a church where you could be caught at any moment.

In *Cigarettes & Wine*, this is where we meet an unnamed teenage narrator in a small southern town trying to make sense of their own bisexuality, gender variance, and emerging adulthood. When our narrator leaves the church, we watch their teenage years unfold alongside one first love wrestling with his own sexuality and his desire for a relationship with God, and another first love seeking to find her self as she moves away from town. Through the narrator's eyes, we also encounter a newly arrived neighbor who appears to be an all American boy, but has secrets and pain hidden behind his charming smile and athletic ability, and their oldest friend who is on the verge of romantic, artistic, and sexual transformations of her own. Along the way, these friends and others they encounter confront questions about gender and sexuality, violence and substance abuse, and the intricacies of love and selfhood in the shadow of churches, families, and a small southern town in the 1990s. Together with the narrator, we walk with them through celebrations and heartaches on the way to adulthood.

Although written as a first-person narrative that allows readers to imagine themselves in the shoes of the narrator, *Cigarettes & Wine* is a novel about relationships and intersections; how the people, places, and stories we encounter in our lives shape the people we become, and the complex ways gender, sexuality, age, religion, region, violence, and broader social norms shape identities, relationships, and experiences. As in life, the themes of relationships and intersections permeate the events captured in the following pages. *Cigarettes & Wine* offers a view into the ways varied intersections and relationships shape and shift the life course over time. It also provides a first person view of the ways churches, families, friends, lovers, and broader social norms influence the efforts of young people seeking to find their place in the world.

Cigarettes & Wine also presents realistic explorations of bisexual and transgender experience all too rarely available in contemporary media or academic materials. Alongside academic and media portrayals of the world that generally only notice binary sexual and gender options, *Cigarettes & Wine* delivers a reminder that non-binary sexual and gender options exist, and introduces readers to some of the conflicts unique to non-binary sexual and gender minorities as well as those shared with other sexual (i.e., gay and lesbian) and gender (i.e., women) minorities in contemporary American society. Especially at a time when even college professors sometimes struggle with topics related to gender and sexual fluidity, *Cigarettes & Wine* supplies readers with a chance to view the world, society, the American south, teenage experience, relationships, and love through the eyes of a non-binary narrator. Readers seeking more information on these subjects may also want to check out, for example, https://bisexual.org/home/ for information on the bisexuality spectrum and http://nonbinary.org/wiki/Main_Page for information on non-binary gender identities.

While entirely fictional, *Cigarettes & Wine* is grounded in my own personal experience as a bisexual (on the pansexual end of the spectrum), genderqueer (formerly identified as a cross-dresser then as trans) person raised in a small South Carolina town. It is also built upon years of ethnographic, auto-ethnographic, historical and statistical research I have done concerning intersections of sexualities, gender, religion, and health in the United States, and hundreds of formal and informal interviews I have conducted – professionally and for personal interest – with bisexual (across the spectrum), transgender and non-binary (across the spectrum), lesbian, gay, asexual, heterosexual, intersex, poly, kink, cisgender and Queer identified people who span the religious-nonreligious spectrum and were raised all over the world. Since stories – both fictional and non-fictional – are often powerful pedagogical tools for stimulating reflection and discussion about even the most challenging topics, I crafted this novel as a way for readers to step into the shoes of a non-binary person, and in so doing, hopefully acquire a starting point for discussion and understanding of sexual and gender complexity in contemporary society.

For me, *Cigarettes & Wine* is a pedagogical text blending my artistic and research endeavors in a manner that has, throughout my career thus far, been incredibly effective in classrooms. In fact, the novel itself developed out of conversations in my own classrooms wherein students – in response to stories I use from my own life and the lives of others I study to illustrate concepts – often suggested I should write a novel so more people would have access to such perspectives within and beyond classrooms. Further, it developed from my own recognition of the ways such stories could have been useful to people like me growing up in a world where explaining bisexual and transgender existence – even to fellow Ph.D. holders – is an exhausting necessity. As such, *Cigarettes & Wine* may be used as an educational tool for people seeking to better understand growing numbers of openly bisexual and transgender people; as a supplemental reading for courses across disciplines dealing with gender, sexualities, relationships, families, religions, the life course, narratives, the American south, identities, culture, and/or intersectionality; or it can, of course, be read entirely for pleasure.

ACKNOWLEDGEMENTS

When I was a kid, I dreamed that one day I would write and publish a novel. To accomplish such a dream, however, requires the help and influence of many people willing to take a chance on a work like this one. I am eternally grateful to each of these people, and especially a subset of them who played important roles in bringing *Cigarettes & Wine* to fruition.

Thank you to Patricia Leavy, Peter de Liefde, Jolanda Karada, Paul Chambers, Robert van Gameren, Edwin Bakker, and everyone else at Sense Publishers and the *Social Fictions* series for your faith in me, your willingness to support creativity, and your invaluable guidance throughout this process. I would also like to thank Shalen Lowell for the considerable assistance and support throughout the submission process. I cannot overstate how much the efforts and support of all of you means to me.

Thank you especially to my life partner Xan Nowakowski for giving me the courage to write this novel in the first place, and walking by my side as I completed it and sent it out for consideration. This book would not exist without your inspiration, guidance, and faith, and I will never be able to thank you enough for what your support and encouragement means to me.

I would also like to thank Lain Mathers, Kate McCabe, Shay Phillips, and Eric Anthony Grollman for providing constructive comments and insights throughout this process, and for being willing to listen to me talk about this project unceasingly while I was writing, editing, and revising it. There is no way for me to adequately express how important your efforts have been to me.

I would also like to thank two people I have never met. This novel emerged as I began listening to the music of Amanda Shires and Jason Isbell, and their records played on a loop throughout the writing, editing, and revising of the novel. As I have written elsewhere, music often fuels my creative and scholarly work, and in this case, their musical stories about life in the south provided part of the fuel for my

ACKNOWLEDGEMENTS

own construction of southern life through the eyes of a bisexual and gender fluid teenager in South Carolina.

Finally, this novel would not be possible without the years of research I have done on sexualities, gender, religion, and health. I have had the privilege of interviewing and observing so many wonderful bisexual, transgender, non-binary, lesbian, gay, intersex, poly, kink, asexual, and otherwise Queer people formally and informally over the years, and many of their experiences find voice throughout this novel. I would thus like to thank all of them both for sharing their stories with researchers like me, and for being role models to many of us navigating sexual and gender fluidity and difference in contemporary society.

CHAPTER 1

We were supposed to be in our weekly Bible Study. We were supposed to be learning about Jesus. We were supposed to be surrounded by other thirteen-year-olds dressed like adults holding Bibles and waiting patiently for the weekly lesson to end. We were supposed to be finishing off the snacks that were always in the larger room before we went into the smaller rooms for the lesson of the week. We were supposed to be taking turns going to the bathroom – otherwise known as finding excuses to leave the room – while the lesson of the week unfolded between the periods of social engagement at the beginning and end of Sunday school.

We were not, however, supposed to be in the little store room on the first floor where they stored the communion wine we did not yet realize was not actually wine. We were not supposed to even know about this particular room I don't think, but we found it one night roaming around the buildings when our usual private spot – the left side of the church library where all the old books no one ever noticed went to die – was occupied for some reason. Or maybe the library was closed that evening. Or maybe we just got bored with the library. I cannot seem to recall for certain what led us to roam around the buildings one evening three weeks before that fateful Sunday, but in any case we found the storeroom with the not really wine that evening and added it to the list of places young people could be alone when we were sent to church for one or another of a collection of social engagements.

In fact, our list had grown rather long over the years. There was the aforementioned left side of the library that was never occupied on Sunday nights when families ate dinner before evening church. There was the suite of rooms where the adults had Sunday school every week that appeared to be completely unmonitored the rest of the week, and actually contained comfortable chairs and sofas perfect for teen imaginations. We sought to see if our own little suite of Sunday school rooms would make a viable setting, but unfortunately it was locked when Sunday school was not in session. It was almost like they didn't trust us to use the space unless we were being spoon fed religious dogma. There were also many other nooks, crannies, and empty rooms located throughout the buildings at any time that was not Sunday morning between seven and noon, but the best by far was the baptismal area.

The baptismal area was located atop the sanctuary within the wall behind where the preacher stood for every sermon. Likely due to its use as a space for dunking people into magical water for a few seconds, it had both a little recessed pool and a perimeter surrounded by padded seating – or kneeling I guess – areas that were quite cozy and rather quiet. We would get together up there to discuss the latest Madonna or Guns N' Roses record or the latest gossip at school. One of the more fascinating aspects of the place was that it was technically closed when not in use. As a result, there was a wood panel that slid across the opening, and created a kind of box that felt extra private. Crafted wooden walls, a tiny little pool, and a set of cushioned seats – I often thought my first sexual experience would and should take place at the holy site of baptism in my childhood church, but that was not the case.

Instead, there I was in a storeroom with the not really wine and sounds from a conversation in the hallway terrifying me to no end. Out in the hallway, one speaker who sounded a whole lot like the music minister at the church was explaining a passage in the Bible where Jesus turns water into wine. Instinctively, my companion and I looked at the boxes of wine wondering if we were about to be visited at any moment. What we could not know at the time – we would find out 45 minutes later in the late worship service – was that the story about the wine had been the centerpiece of the week's morning service. Rather than impending doom, my partner in crime and I were simply listening to the same rehashing of the sermon topic that seemed to follow every service. Someone who was either actually curious or seeking to look good in the church had cornered the music minister in search of further discussion on the topic, and neither had any clue – to the best of my knowledge then and now – they were rudely interrupting an initial foray into oral sex.

Over the years, I have realized that very few things can induce the level of quiet in young people as the possibility that an older person is about to catch them doing something fun. As we waited in the storeroom for the conversation outside to end or for the minister to catch us, I remember trying to count just how many rules we were currently breaking. First, there was the sin of skipping Sunday school, which in and of itself was worthy of scorn in that church. Second, there was the act of breaking into a storeroom that we were neither supposed to know about or use for any reason. Third, there was the fact that we were basically taught that sexual activity was dirty, wrong, and against God unless it happened in marriage and only for the purposes of creating screaming little humans, which only made us all the more curious about it as we grew up under the roof of that place. Fourth, fifth, sixth…I could go on, but needless to say I started thinking I might need a calculator if we were caught.

I also realized much later just how many major moments in my life involved a mixture of excitement and fear contained within an enclosed space that I was not supposed to be in at the time. How many times had I walked into this room or that one for one purpose or another, and come out transformed by a new or just unexpected turn of events? I don't know if I can count that high. So much of my early life took place in private spaces carved out by a constant tension between what the people in that little town expected and what was really happening behind the scenes. I didn't think of any of these things at the moment, but rather, I just sat there in the storeroom wondering whether or not we would get caught.

We were not caught. After a few minutes of conversation that can only be described as utterly boring, the people said goodbye, and slowly the voices dissipated. As soon as they did, my partner in crime finally started breathing again, and said, "Well, that was not fun." I distinctly remember I could not help myself, it was not my fault, I had no control over myself at the moment. I started laughing like a lunatic. My companion did not share my enjoyment, and kept telling me to be quiet until finally I got all the laughter out. All I could think to say was, "Well, this was your idea," and I started laughing again.

It had been his idea. We were sitting in Sunday school a few months back when he noticed me staring at the picture of Jesus that hung in the room. While everyone was socializing after the lesson, he came over to me, and asked, "Why do you stare at the Jesus picture in class?" The truth of the matter was that I simply loved Jesus' hair and body, and thought he was just so cute, but this was a conservative Christian church in a small town in the south so I said, "I don't know. I guess I just like it." I had, however, also seen him looking at the picture and at me before so I asked, "What do you think?"

This simple exchange began a series of small conversations between the two of us about Jesus and life that continued until the day after we shared our special moment in the storeroom. We would team up when we met on Monday nights for youth volleyball, walk together back and forth to get milkshakes from the diner nearby, sit together in Sunday school and church, and pass each other notes each week when we got to Sunday school. Like many childhood crushes, I question my taste in hindsight, but at the time he seemed very sweet and funny. More importantly, he seemed curious and that was an important quality for me at the time.

One night we were sitting downstairs in the game room below the gym where weekly volleyball happened, and he asked me if I had ever kissed anybody. I told him I had, but I had not done any other stuff. You gotta keep in mind that for a small town kid "stuff" may as well have been the official linguistic marker for anything not shown on local television before bed time. He admitted that he had never been kissed, and so I gave him one and watched him react with a mixture of fascination, embarrassment, and fear of being caught by any of the people upstairs playing volleyball. We kissed a few more times on a few more occasions before he asked me what other stuff I wanted to do.

I don't really know why, but at the time I was fascinated by what I called "boy parts." I thought they were just the ideal of cute, and I wanted to snuggle them like one of my stuffed animals. I remember one time an older boy just whipped his out in the front yard, and started swinging his hips. I was transfixed. All I could do was stare, and when his mother made him put it away, I wanted him to pull it back out. I remember his girlfriend – who I was friends with – apologizing to me about it, but I thought it was one of the greatest days of my life. That little thing – and honestly the boy too – was just so damn cute.

I told my companion this story, and then I told him that one of the older boys had told me that it felt good when he got kissed down there. As I hoped, my companion became intrigued with this idea, and we talked about it regularly for the next couple weeks until one night we were roaming around the buildings of the church with other kids and stumbled across the storeroom with the wine we did not know was not really wine. As the other people slowly disappeared that night, one by one, having to go be picked up to leave, he and I remained sitting on the floor in the little room. As we got ready to leave for our own rides, he softly said, "We could come here and try the kissing thing one day if you want." I didn't respond, but deep inside me somewhere I was only starting to get to know, I really liked this idea.

And that was how we ended up in this little room starting to calm down after being scared by fellow churchgoers. After my laughter finally subsided, he smiled at me and asked me what I wanted to do. Very softly, a little nervous I admit, I said, "I want to kiss you…there." He said, "Me too," and I leaned over and undid his nice enough for church but too nice for anything else pants slowly. I remember being surprised that it was so soft and small. I had only seen a couple of them at this point in my life, and the others had been harder looking and bigger. I remember wondering just how many sizes and colors and shapes these things came in, and for some reason, I started thinking that maybe they were like baseball cards or stuffed animals or something else where people try to collect all the different editions. I wondered how long it would take to get a full set, and if there was a Becket guide for that type of thing. I almost started laughing again at the thought, but fought to maintain a straight face. At least as much for fun as to stifle potential laughter, I began my sexual life.

A little while later, he began to convulse and pulled back from me. He was shaking. I was confused. The room was silent. It was over. Without a word, he re-buckled his pants, and stood – almost knocking me over – to pull up his zipper. The only thing he said was, "I, uh, I think it's time for church," before leaving the room. I sat there for a few minutes trying to figure out what happened. One minute he seemed very happy, and the next minute he was rushing out of the room as if the devil showed up to visit us or maybe the music minister decided to check out the wine that was not actually wine after all. I would spend the entire church service and the rest of the day trying to figure it out, and come up with nothing. At the same time, I spent the rest of the day thinking about how much fun it was, and what it might be like the next time we were alone together. Unfortunately, I never learned the answer to that particular question.

Instead, the next night at volleyball my companion acted like I was not there, and spent his time talking with other people. About halfway through the evening, I finally went over to him and said hello. Instead of the warm hellos I had begun to look forward to, he quietly said hi and then went back to talking to other people. I didn't know what was happening, and we never had another conversation like the ones we had before that day in the storeroom. I still have no way of knowing exactly what happened to him in that moment, but I think I'll always remember that day and the other times he showed up in my life even if I never can bring myself to say his name again.

CHAPTER 2

"You kissed him like that," Jordan says a little too loud after hearing what happened at church. "Really, you did that? Did you like it?"

Jordan does not go to my church. We met when I was eight, and became fast friends because we lived not too far from each other, both played soccer at the fields near our neighborhoods, and both loved music. Jordan is a few months older than I am. He will, in fact, never let me forget this little tidbit. I live in the neighborhood on the north side of the park where most of the sports in the area are played by children and adults with dreams of getting out of this little town. Jordan lives on the south side of the same park in the neighborhood that houses the football stadium used for peewee and middle school games. We meet at the park regularly throughout most of my childhood.

Our little town is like so many others that circle Augusta, Georgia. A couple of hours from Atlanta and about an hour from Columbia, Augusta is the biggest game we have as we grow up in our little enclaves. We live in one of the towns across the river in South Carolina nestled amid our neighbors with names like Clearwater, Edgefield, North Augusta, Jackson, Johnston, and Graniteville. Towns built on factory work and long abandoned mills populated with more churches than anything else it seems. The other side of the river, circling the city in its own way, holds similar little places like Hephzibah, Wrens, Waynesboro, Queens, Louisville, and Grovetown. The whole area becomes the center of national attention every year when the Master's golf tournament begins, and crowds of media and tourists arrive, but the rest of the time it's a sleepy little area not unlike many other places in the south. Like so many other kids in our little town and others we meet over the years, we dream of the day we live somewhere else while also maintaining an awareness that very few people actually ever leave.

Stuttering and not at all sounding as cool as I want to in the moment, I say, "Yeah...I mean, I don't know...I mean, kind of yeah I think so." Jordan just laughs.

Jordan was at camp when the events occurred, and has just returned. This summer will be the last one he spends at camp, but neither of us know that yet. I could not wait to tell the story, and find out someone else's thoughts, but decisions about how to tell someone about your first sexual experience have to be navigated with caution in small towns in the south and maybe in other places as well. Naturally, I went to Jordan because we talk about everything, always have, well, always since we were eight and eight-and-a-half respectively. Jordan continues to laugh, and reaches into his pockets for a box of cigarettes.

"You want a smoke," he says.

"Where did you get cigarettes? When did you start smoking?"

"They had them at the camp, some of the older people did it so I tried one. They're kind of nice – helps me turn off the ole brain, mate," he says tapping me on the shoulder.

Jordan lights a smoke, and I watch his firm forearm curl and release for just a minute. I am in love with Jordan. Jordan knows this. I know Jordan knows this, and I think Jordan loves me too, but he has never really said so explicitly. I have been in love with Jordan since the first day he walked onto the field for our first match against each other. Jordan knows this too. Jordan knows a lot of things that other people do not know about me. I am pretty sure Jordan is the perfect creation, and the only possible reason I might ever believe in a god. Jordan knows this as well. He also knows that beside him I feel like a blithering idiot, but he assures me I am beautiful in my own way and somehow makes me believe him.

"What the hell is a mate," I ask still watching him. The smoke softly escapes his lips, and he squeezes the cigarette in his fingers, those perfect fingers. He takes another puff, and blows it out like he's been doing this for years.

"It's like guy or man or whatever – it just means buddy or friend or what not. Damn, you are always asking questions."

This is true. I am always asking questions. I'm, as my parents used to say, addicted to curiosity. Punching him in the arm, I say, "And what's wrong with that MATE."

Laughing, he smiles and says, "So you kind of think you might have liked giving a blowjob?" He chuckles and takes another drag off his cigarette.

"A blowjob?"

"It's what they call it when you kiss a guy down there dumbass."

"Did you learn that at camp from your mates?"

"Nah, I got that from one of mom's "adult" magazines," he says before taking another puff from his cigarette. "Kind of cool you did it at the church I gotta admit, but I guess I'm not your first anymore" he says before messing up my hair.

Jordan was my first kiss. I was eight. He was adamantly eight and a half. We had just finished our first soccer match against each other, and one of his teammates invited our team to walk over to the concession stand and hang out. I admit that I mainly went to hang out with Jordan, and that I basically thought all the other boys were losers. I was dribbling a ball off to the side of the stand, ignoring the crowd of loud and smelly soccer players I already felt like I spent too much time with, when Jordan came over and took the ball. Jerk – I chased him across the park for what felt like an hour to an eight year old, and tackled him with all the strength I had in the little field right before the park turns into the woods.

"What do you mean you're not my first now?" This thought really bothers me for reasons I can't quite put into words.

Throwing out his cigarette, he nods sagely – always the older expert – and says, "Well, sex counts more to guys than kissing so now that dude is your first."

"That's stupid as hell!"

"I don't know, maybe now you belong to him and I should just leave you alone," he says with that little smile he had the day he stole my ball.

After I tackled him, we wrestled in the grass for a minute, and I proudly informed him that he was a jerk. Instead of being offended, he kissed me. Right on the lips, right there at the park, right out of the blue, he kissed me! I could have killed him, but I wanted him to do it again. It was a new feeling, I mean, I felt like I was melting so I did the only thing I could think of – I punched him in the face and told him never to do that again. It made sense at the time, I promise. He just laughed and held his jaw for a few minutes in the grass. After a few minutes, he leaned in again, and this time I kissed him too, and I didn't stop for years. Neither did he.

"Don't be a jerk, mate," I say and shove him against the fence on the side of the path after we have fully entered the woods and left the park behind for the moment.

Smiling, he says, "I don't know, I don't want to be fighting with some other dude over you from here on out." With that, he leans in slowly and softly kisses me on the lips and wraps his arms around me. Our lips combine in a form of music that shakes me inside even when I think about it all these years later. We sway back and forth, sharing the moment, and holding onto each other for dear life.

After a few minutes, my voice cracks as I say, "I missed you."

"I missed you too."

We stand there in silence holding each other for a few more minutes. The same way we have for years already at that point, we both know that something between us is powerful and important. At the same time, we go to different schools, different churches, and different neighborhoods when we leave the woods. We dance this way together for a decade – somewhat together, somewhat separate – but in the heat of these shared moments we both somehow know that nothing can really ever separate us. The world beyond the woods may never know it, but we know it with all we are.

"So," he whispers as his head rests on my shoulder, "You kind of liked it?"

"Yeah, it was nice, it was fun, but it was also strange."

"What was strange about it?"

"I don't know really, but at some point he felt like he got really happy, but then he kind of ran away and he hasn't really spoken to me since."

"Asshole."

"Yep, but he wasn't before then so I don't understand what happened."

"I'd guess he got freaked out. Maybe he isn't ready for this type of stuff. The first person I was with, you know, like that, was amazing, but I totally freaked out and could not get home fast enough. Remember, I faked being sick so my mom would come get me early?"

I did remember that. I remembered that at camp last summer Jordan met someone nice who he really liked, and they had sex like

I did in the storeroom. I remembered that it hurt. I remembered that Jordan came home early, and I thought he wouldn't like me anymore. I remembered that he came home and said he missed me. I remembered that he said sex was scary, that he didn't know if he would do it again, that he didn't like it. I remembered wanting to make him feel better, but not knowing what to do. I remembered he didn't talk about it much. I remembered that I tried not to remember all these things because they still hurt for some reason.

"Well, I was a mess. I got so freaked out, and it wasn't anything that they did, you know? I just wasn't ready, and so it was scary as hell. I was at camp, I was horny, I didn't know what I was doing, and it just happened kind of out of the blue before I really thought about it. I just freaked out so maybe that's what happened to your guy."

"Maybe, still sucks."

"I know. Do you like him?"

"I mean, I did like him, I mean, not like I like you, but I did like him. I don't know, I was lonely and kind of sad and kind of curious, I don't know."

"Yep, that's kind of how I was," and with that he kissed me on my head, and we started walking again.

"How was camp this year?"

"Same old boring shit, but I guess my mom needs the vacation."

Jordan had gone to camp of some sort every summer I had known him. His mom was all alone raising him, and he thought the camps were kind of like a summer babysitter service. His dad disappeared at some point before he could remember, and his mom wasn't welcome in her family because she got pregnant out of wedlock with Jordan. It was just the two of them against the world, but as his mom often said, "The world usually won." Jordan helped her as much as he could, but things were tight and she was always tired from work, from neighbors, from life, or just in general. I don't think I ever saw her once without wondering how she even kept going when she never seemed to be happy for even a second.

After a few minutes walking down the path, Jordan stops and stares out at the woods. He lights a cigarette, and just stares out at nothing. Softly, I ask, "Are you okay?"

11

"I don't like you messing around with other people."

"I don't like you messing around with other people either Jordan."

"I know, neither do I."

"Same here."

We just stand there silently for a few minutes. Jordan's cigarette breathes all around us, and he touches my cheek. His hand smells like cigarettes. It reminds me of my grandmother and my best friend Abs and happy times on back porches. It reminds me of the older kids in the neighborhood sitting on the hoods of cars at night, and letting me tag along because they all know Lena. It reminds me of how Lena hides her cigarettes from her parents in an old box on her back porch. It reminds me of things that we hide because other people would not approve. He takes another puff, lowers his hand, and sighs. I grab his hand, and he smiles just a little bit. "I don't like it," he says, "but I don't know what else to do. I don't know what else to do."

"I don't either," I say and we smile at each other. Without another word, we start walking back to the park hands grasped tight, voices silent in the emerging night, and trying to figure out this thing called love.

CHAPTER 3

Early that fall, I had another kind of sex for the first time. It did not occur at church. It did not end with one of us running out of the room. It did not lead to ceased communications between the two of us. It did not involve wine that was not actually wine. It did not involve any scary moment where we thought we might get caught. In fact, I somehow managed to avoid all of the negative aspects of my other first experience this time around, and yet, it still began in a rather awkward manner.

"What are you doing in my closet silly," Lena asked as she entered her bedroom faster than I expected. She had left to feed her dog, which – without any point of reference at the time – I expected to take quite a while. It did not. I froze. I did not know what to say. What reason would a thirteen-year-old boy have to be looking through the closet of a sixteen-year-old girl? What could I possibly be looking for? What, if any, excuse would make sense in this context? My usually quick wit failed me miserably.

Luck, however, had other plans. I turned around, stepped out of the closet, and looked to see Lena smiling at me. Wait, why is she smiling, I thought. This was no simple smile, she was grinning from ear to ear. What the hell was going on? Why is she happy about finding me in her closet? I still had nothing by way of an excuse, but for some reason she looked, I don't know, happy, I mean, really happy?

"I, uh, well, I," nice job supposedly smart kid. Oh hell, I thought, I'm dead now, but Lena just started laughing for some reason. Okay, maybe this moment is a little bit like the storeroom with what's his name. Maybe she sees something hilarious in my fear that I cannot quite grasp. So, I'm what's his name, and she's me, okay, what is the funny thing I can't see. I tried for a few seconds that felt like hours to figure it out, but I came up with nothing – not even a good guess. What was she laughing at?

"So you are a real boy after all aren't you," she giggled at me and fell to one knee laughing.

I met Lena when I was about five years old according to her. Lena was well known in my neighborhood the whole time she lived there. She was sweet, smart, sexy, and just plain beautiful. Obviously, parents hated her. Just as obviously, all the kids loved her. According to the legend as she told it, I stumbled into her yard when I was five-years-old looking for my mommy, and crying for some reason that was never made clear. My mom used to have a friend that lived in the house between Lena's and Abs' place on the block, and sadly, this made the legend more plausible than I cared to admit as I got older. Three years my senior, Lena thought I was just adorable. She said I was this perfect, silly, little sad creature. She still called me silly, but the origin story for that term had a few different versions. She scooped me up in her arms, and held me while I cried and we had been friends ever since. From then on, we hung out a lot and she told me all the stories a girl growing up pretty in a small southern town has to tell, and I told her almost everything too. I was the only person – other than her most trusted girlfriends of course – who knew when she had intercourse for the first time, first got kissed, first smoked a cigarette, and first tried "Drugs that you should never do because they're bad." At the same time, she was the only person who knew I was in love with Jordan and had even kissed him many times. We were buddies, we had fun.

I stared at her, and could only say, "What," but I knew what she meant.

Lena had always teased me about falling in love with another boy. She thought it was cute, but also not really good. Keep in mind, this was much better than the eternal damnation promised by my church, the nuclear options suggested by class and team mates over the years, and the disgust that seemed to cross the face of everyone else I knew every time an example of "the homos" showed up on television or otherwise. That said, I knew exactly what she meant by "real boy," and she had already trained me pretty well for the many people I would meet throughout my life that could not understand that I liked boys, girls, and everyone in between rather than only boys or only girls and especially only girls.

Smiling and finally not laughing so hard, Lena said, "Oh, you're just curious, and that is great, but honey, if you wanted to see my panties all you had to do was ask." With that, she pulled her pants down just a little bit, and showed me the top of a lovely pair of black panties. They looked like they might be silk, and I stared for a minute wondering what they would feel like on my body. I started to think about what I might wear them with, but my mind quickly came back to the moment and her reaction to my exploration of her closet.

Things were now starting to make sense, kind of. She, for some reason, thought I was looking in her closet to see her panties. Okay, this was somewhat true, but not quite. In reality, I was looking in her closet imagining what I would look like if I felt safe enough to wear her clothes. She had so many amazing outfits, and I liked to picture myself in them when we were hanging out so I thought, with her moving soon, I would get a good look at all of them for posterity sake. One of the main reasons I enjoyed Lena was because hanging out with her allowed me to be – almost – as girly as I wanted to be. I was imagining myself as a girl, thinking about what my wardrobe would be if I became a girl, and touching the pretty clothes. I guess I could have told her this, but at the moment, that did not seem like the smartest play.

Instead, I said, "Well I've always told you I like girls and boys." Of course, at that time I didn't know there were many other options, but later in life I would learn I like all of them as well. For whatever reason, the things people call sex, genitals, gender, and such never really had any impact on who I wanted to touch and be close to. I'm not sure why this is, but by the time I was a teenager I had already begun to accept it. Instead of telling Lena about my fantasies involving her clothes, I just said, "I guess I just got curious, I'm sorry."

At this point, she walked across the room, and said, "Oh honey that is okay, its perfectly natural to be curious," and gave me a hug. I admit I was a little stunned. How was it perfectly natural to want to sneak into a girl's closet to look at her panties in a sexual way?

My best friend would actually explain this to me at church a couple days later. Her name was Abigail but we all called her Abs, and she was always good for information because she kind of seemed to know everything about everything. Apparently, it was some kind of right of passage to steal a girl's panties, and it was so well known that it was kind of seen as a normal part of growing up to be a man. I still think this sounds incredibly creepy personally, but Abs assured me that it was not all that unusual at the time and even told me stories of other boys in our Sunday school class who had done similar things already.

While Lena held me in her arms, she asked, "So does this have to do with that boy you had sex with over the summer?" Lena was the only person other than Jordan and what's his name who knew this little detail, and I wasn't really sure how it was relevant, but I decided to go with it. After all, Lena's boyfriend was the one who told me guys liked it when they got kissed like that, and Lena confirmed this message at the time. For the most part, until the last few seconds in the storeroom, they had been right about that one.

"I don't know. Maybe, uh, that was just really strange."

"Oh I bet it was honey, you're just all confused."

I didn't know it at the time, but I was going to have to get used to this phrase. People like me apparently confuse the hell out of everybody else, and their response is to usually suggest that we must be confused because we haven't developed the same sexual desires they have. I have no clue why this is, but apparently when someone is different from what you expect, a common response is to suggest that they are the one who has the problem instead of asking why you never considered a person like them before. I didn't know it at the time, but this would be the first time I remembered hearing the phrase, and I remember even in this case it felt incredibly insulting in a way I still have trouble putting into words.

Pulling back from me just a few inches, Lena said, "You know what you need?"

I honestly figured neither of us had any clue what I needed at that moment. Part of me thought I needed a way out of this conversation, and part of me thought I needed a way to steal Lena's clothes and move to some city where I could be a girl or at least dress like one sometimes. I just kind of stared at her trying to figure out what she thought I needed. I drew a blank. At the moment, my only source of comfort was the fact that Lena was moving soon. Her father had taken a job in Atlanta, and that's where her mother and father were on this fateful day. The same piece of information that gave me the courage to investigate her clothes and makeup made me feel much better about this incredibly awkward situation. She knew way too much – about Jordan, about what's his name, about my interest in girl's clothes, about how girly I could be – but soon she would be gone so all I had to do was stay quiet and get through this moment.

So, that's what I did. I just stared into her eyes and said nothing. I did this for what seemed like forever, for as long as I could, and then I got too nervous and I looked down. Apparently, this was another signal I was unaware of because right as I looked down, she smiled and said, "Exactly, you need a girl."

I was stunned. I said the only thing I could think of at the moment, "Lena, I have a girlfriend, you know that."

I may have been in love with Jordan and perfectly willing to be with only Jordan at the time, but neither of us thought that was a good idea in our small town. Since I also liked girls, I had, with Jordan's support, started dating – talking on the phone, hanging out at school, a bit of kissing, you know the drill – a really nice girl from my church and my school. She was great, we had a lot of fun and I liked her a lot. I told Lena all about her, and how much fun I had with her. I even asked Lena if it was possible to love two people instead of one because of how I felt about this girl and Jordan. I had a girl and Lena knew that so what was she talking about? How could I need something I already had, and what did that have to do with looking at panties in a clandestine manner? I had to admit it – I was kind of confused in the moment.

Lena, however, was unfazed. She chuckled and twisted the end of one of the pieces of her shiny red hair, smiled at me in a way I had not seen before, and lightly waved her finger in a side-to-side motion. As she moved her finger, she asked, "Have you had sex with this girlfriend?" She always said "this girlfriend" because I don't think Lena thought my girlfriend was real. She knew my girlfriend existed, but she didn't seem to take it seriously for some reason I didn't really understand. As usual, I was more than mildly annoyed by the phrase, but I wanted to get out of this moment so I ignored it to the best of my abilities.

"No, I told you. I only had sex with that one guy."

"Exactly, you need a girl."

Suddenly, things started to really make sense. Lena, literally the most attractive person I had ever seen in real life (my apologies even to Jordan on this one, but even Abs agreed with me here), was suggesting I have sex with a girl, with her maybe, I wasn't sure, but I was intrigued. The only problem was that I didn't know what it meant to have sex with a girl. What do you do? Is there a girl version of kissing "down there"? Lena had done something called intercourse, but I only vaguely thought I might know what that actually was at that point in my young life. I heard older kids talking about getting some, but I wasn't exactly sure what that was since all the television shows and movies just showed kissing followed by commercials. I never bothered to look at the "adult" magazines Jordan talked about and his mom apparently enjoyed. At thirteen, I literally knew nothing about sex with a girl. I didn't know much about sex with boys either actually, but what little I did know didn't, that I know of, have to do with girls. The mechanics were a complete mystery to me to say the least. In that moment, I realized it was a real problem – I didn't know how to have sex with a girl even though I knew that I really did want to at some point. Why had this not crossed my mind before this moment?

In another stroke of luck, Lena knew exactly what she was doing. Stepping back from me, she said, "Sit down on the bed, and relax." I didn't know what to say or do so I just obeyed and hoped for the best.

As I sat down, Lena pulled her pink tank top over her head, and threw it on the floor. At first, I felt a little nervous, and started to blush and lower my head. Lena stepped forward, raised my head, and whispered, "It's okay to watch," as she undid and removed her black bra. She then put her hands in her pants, and rubbed back and forth for a few seconds. She told me to lie back on the bed, and she crawled up between my legs smiling like she knew some secret I had yet to learn. She began rubbing me, and I felt myself start to stiffen the way I did in the shower when I touched myself, the way I had with what's his name, the way I did when Jordan kissed me, the way I did when my girlfriend kissed me. I began to breathe deeper and deeper, and Lena began unbuckling my belt.

The next thing I knew my belt was on the floor, and she asked, "Do you feel okay silly?" I nodded that I did, and she said, "We don't have to do this if you don't want to." I'll never forget those words or how beautiful they sounded in my ears at that moment. Lena did not understand my sexual desires. Lena did not understand that I felt like I was a girl in some ways. I was pretty sure Lena did not fully accept me for who I felt like I was, even though later in life she would. But Lena did care about me. Lena did want me to feel good. Lena did want me to be treated well. Lena did want to make sure I was ready, that I was sure, before doing what she wanted to do to me.

I nodded and said, "Yes, I'm sure." As soon as I stopped speaking, she began doing things to my body, and I wondered why I had not thought of many of these things with what's his name. I began to take notes in my head of everything Lena did. I wanted to be like her in yet another way. It seemed like a long time, but like in the storeroom, it only took a little bit before I began to convulse the same way what's his name had. It scared me, but it felt good. Lena stopped, and asked, "Do you want me to stop?"

Once again, I wondered why I had not thought of that. At the same time, I did not want her to stop. The convulsions were scary, but they also felt good. It was like the way it felt when I was alone, but stronger, more intense, more immediate, more full bodied, I guess. When I was alone it led to good things and I assumed this would be a similar process so what was the harm. I decided to go for it. I said, "No, I'm okay. Keep going if you want to." Lena kept going, and going, until I told her I was going to make a mess. I don't know why that was what it was called in my head, but that's what ejaculating meant to me. When I told her that, Lena said, "Thanks for warning me silly," between punctuated giggles – apparently make a mess was funny so I took a note not to say it that way again.

When she was finished, Lena went to the bathroom down the hall and brought back a towel. I don't know how long she was gone because I could not really feel my legs. I felt very relaxed and sleepy. Everything seemed to be moving in slow motion. Lena used the towel to clean us up, and then said she was going out for a smoke. I laid there for what seemed like a very long time. I stared at the glow-in-the-dark stars on her ceiling. I was in a kind of trance. At some point, I rolled over and saw her Madonna poster on the wall. It was the one that was so common back then where Madonna seems to be reclining with her neck and back arched in pleasure. I could relate to that poster. I remembered Lena saying that poster would be the last thing to leave this room before her, and I suddenly felt even worse about her pending departure. I wondered what she was doing, so I got up and went out to the back porch.

She was sitting on the porch smoking a cigarette and sipping a purple liquid from a glass. I suddenly felt very shy, very small, maybe like a five-year-old who has lost his mommy. "Can I sit with you," I asked and noticed my voice was trembling.

She looked up at me and smiled. "Now, don't get weird silly, you're still my favorite youngin'. Sadly, I can't say I care half as much about some of the others I have done that with as I do about you, so yes come here and hang out." I sat down beside her like I had for so long. "I'm going to miss this place, you know? I'm going to miss you and the guys and school. Atlanta better be fun." She took a sip of her drink, and I did too. It was the wine she hid under her bed for special occasions, and I wondered if it was me or leaving that was the occasion this time. The combination of the wine and cigarettes hit my nostrils, and made me smile for some reason.

"Do you really have to go?"

"Yeah, dad says it's an opportunity, and I never planned to live here when I was older anyway, so yeah, I gotta go. How do you feel?"

"Really good and kind of tired."

"Good. Did you like it?"

"Yes, a lot, did you?"

"Definitely, I learned that when I was younger, and I've always loved it. I know you're probably still confused, but I don't think Jordan can make you feel like this." My face must have said something because she said, "That's just what I think silly. I could be wrong, but I just don't think it can be the same between two boys."

"I don't know. I still love Jordan and I think I might love Jessica too. It's kind of like you and me, you know, but it's not the same either."

"Ah, Jessica, yeah you probably should not tell her or Jordan about today."

"Why not?"

"Silly, not everyone is as open minded as I am. Jessica – and many other girlfriends you might have – might not want you touching other girls or Jordan. Isn't that why you haven't told her about Jordan?"

"Kind of, but also because we don't really tell anyone about us."

"Well, this is another thing you should probably keep to yourself." I remember thinking in that moment that the list of such things was starting to get kind of long.

"Okay," I said knowing that I would tell Jordan and not sure what I would do about Jessica. "How did you learn to do it?"

Laughing and putting out her cigarette before lighting another one, "Oh silly boy, it just takes practice. I was just as dreadful as you think you were the first time – I felt like an idiot, but I liked it so I did it again. You just practice and it gets easier. There are also all kinds of other things you can do. Mitch and I got books about it from the magazine shop and tried all kinds of stuff over the summer. It's a lot of fun, but just takes practice. Who knows, maybe I'll teach you a few things before I say goodbye." She took a sip of her wine. I took a sip of her wine. She puffed on her cigarette. I watched her smoke. I had no clue just how accurate her words were.

We sat on the porch for a few more hours, just like we had many times before and just like we would a few more times before she moved away. We talked about the same old topics. We laughed at the same old jokes. We made fun of the same old people we always had. And, at times, we just sat and stared out at the woods in the distance beyond her backyard. We drank wine, she smoked cigarettes, and we began the process of saying goodbye to our time as childhood neighbors without a care in the world.

CHAPTER 4

"I don't know how you can say that. The New Kids on the Block are not a band! Pink Floyd is a band," Jessica says after taking a sip of her drink.

Becca scoffs, and says, "You just don't get it Jess, old music is nothing compared to the new stuff coming out."

This is a recurring argument. Becca loves everything pop and Jessica thinks pop music should be burned on sight for the most part. We're having lunch by the little tree near the basketball courts at school, and as is often the case, the conversation revolves around the two of them arguing while the rest of us laugh or smile like a dutiful audience. Within a few minutes, if the script continues on its normal course, Becca will finally become aggravated enough to storm off from the table, and everyone will laugh and shift to another subject until she ultimately returns five minutes later with an ice cream cone from the cantina as if nothing happened.

Jessica is my girlfriend. That still seems odd to say on the day in question, but it is in fact quite a pleasant experience for young me. I never had a girlfriend before, and I did not know anything about the girlfriends I would have in the years to come, but somehow even then I felt like Jessica was an important part of my life. It all started when Becca – who basically lives next to Jessica at any moment they are not on the phone with each other – came over to me during one of the pre-lesson group social gathering times at Sunday school. Smiling in a way I would come to later realize meant she was up to something, Becca said, "Jessica likes you."

I remember first thinking this had to be a joke of some sort. Jessica was almost the opposite of everyone in my life. Her family had college degrees. She lived in the bigger houses in the nicer neighborhoods in town. She had never been in any trouble anywhere at all that I knew of at that point. Her parents drove new cars that looked like the ones I saw on television commercials. She made good grades, and barely spoke at school. No one I saw her with smoked, tried drugs, drank, or even cursed yet from what I could tell. She was one of the good kids as the adults said at the time.

As such, I just repeated Becca's statement with less certainty, "Jessica likes...me?"

Complicating matters for me was the fact that I had never spoken more than three words to Jessica. I realized that all I really knew about her was that she was one of the good kids, she had really beautiful light brown hair, and the way her voice seemed to switch octaves unexpectedly when she spoke really intrigued me. In fact, at the moment I realized that I was also currently having the longest conversation I ever had with Becca. I looked across the room, and saw Jessica standing against the wall in a pale yellow button down shirt looking anywhere but in the direction of Becca and I.

"Hello, yes, she likes you. You should give me your number so she can call you and y'all can go out."

Automatically, I thought about Jordan. Is that what Jordan and I did, went out? I didn't really know, and made a mental note to ask him. At the same time, I remembered sitting by the river with Jordan a few weeks earlier talking about a different girl I was interested in. Jordan did not seem to understand liking both boys and girls, but he said that if I liked someone I should try it out. Should I try it out? Here was a girl who liked me, should I see what that was like? She was very pretty, and I was months away from the confusion generated by a given Sunday morning in a storeroom and an unexpected new experience in Lena's bedroom. At the moment, it seemed like a fun thing to try out, so I gave Becca my number.

From that moment, I somehow became part of this little group that I now ate lunch with everyday at school. Jessica and I began talking on the phone regularly, and I found that I really liked her. She was one of the good kids so to speak, but there was a lot more there too. She was fascinated with music, and her mom had an amazing record collection. I would walk the path – the same one that hit the park south of my house – north from my house and across a few neighborhoods to the area where she lived. I would stare at all the two and three story houses, and wonder what it was like to live in that neighborhood. I would tell Jordan about these things as we cuddled in the grass, walked by the river, and made out in the woods. Jordan thought Jessica sounded good for me, but also felt a little jealous that her and I could go out while him and I were left in the woods.

Over the summer, while Jordan was at camp, Jessica and I – sometimes with Becca along for the ride no matter how annoying she got – would go swimming in the river, and a couple times I was invited to dinners with her parents. They did not care for me for any number of reasons, but that only seemed to make Jessica like me even more. We would listen to Jodeci, Marvin Gaye, and Pink Floyd on her couch, steal kisses when her parents were at work, touch each other in all kinds of ways that were new to both of us, and talk about the world beyond our little town. Over time, I came to realize that Jessica and her friends were both very different from the people in my neighborhood and very similar at the same time. They might not talk about cigarettes, alcohol, or drugs yet, but they were curious about music, love, sex, and the future. They might have bigger houses and more stuff, but they were curious, scared, and uncertain teenagers just like the rest of us. Some of them were wonderful, and some of them were jerks – just like the people in my neighborhood. I found both the differences and the similarities fascinating, and at times, felt like I was simply studying all the different ways people could be people.

The day I found out Jordan had sex at camp, Jessica invited me over to hang out. I crawled into her lap, and cried for a little while. When she asked why I was upset, I told her I got into a fight with my parents, and left it at that. Jessica knew all too well how easy it was to fight with parents, and she never pushed me for details. I loved her in that moment, but I also felt guilty for lying to her. I also felt sad, but at the time I didn't understand why. Looking back after other relationships, I realize that the sadness came from the knowledge that I could never fully connect to her or Jordan as long as I kept things from either one of them. At the time, I didn't understand that – I just knew she made me feel things like Jordan did. At the same time, she also made me feel things Jordan did not and Jordan also made me feel things she did not.

Months later, sitting around the table as Becca returned with her ice cream cone, there were even more things Jessica did not know. She did not know about the storeroom, and I had not told her about Lena. She still did not know about Jordan. She did not know I sometimes dressed up like a girl and pretended or wished I was one. She did not really ever know me, but at that time I really wanted her to for reasons I still cannot put into words.

CHAPTER 5

Where I grew up, some people began accessing and utilizing the Internet in the early 1990s. The rest of us often drew on local book, record, and magazine shops for information. There was one of these shops not too far from my house. Instead of heading south for the park, I would head east through the neighborhood, the opposite direction of the river, until I reached the main road that ran from the interstate highway on the far east end of town to the train yards situated on the far west end of town. As I strolled through the neighborhood, usually enjoying whichever rap cassette I had in my Walkman at the time, I watched the families, looked at the lawns, and listened to the muffled sounds coming from inside the series of one-story ranch style houses that populated my neighborhood.

When I got to the main road, I turned toward the west end of town, crossed the road, and walked another 1.5 miles to a little shopping center that held a grocery store, a pizza delivery place, a drug store, and the jackpot that was the source of music and reading materials. The place was no more than a little storefront the size of a car or two. When you walked inside, automatically, you were met with a check out desk on the right and a wall of cassette tapes for sale on the left side. About four feet into the room – I mean, really, it was a store in name, but basically just a little room in terms of space, hell, Lena's closet was actually about the same size to my young eyes – the magazine racks began with a few paperbacks here and there. I almost always headed to the back corner right away.

In the back corner, the owner stocked a selection of fashion and women's magazines that always seemed to have the most amazing pictures, advice columns, and feature stories for those of us trying to learn to be modern American women. I would spend hours over the years reading every issue I could get my hands on. I would learn from these writers how to properly apply this or that makeup I wished I was brave enough to wear. I would learn how to talk like a lady, walk like a lady, dress like a lady, and handle the boys like Madonna or Janet Jackson. I would learn what types of blush looked good with what types of outfits, and what types of makeup sent the wrong message. I remember wondering what the wrong message was, but the magazines never seemed to explain this outright. I figured maybe other girls learned that from their sisters and moms or something. I would dig through the issues imagining myself as the cover model, thinking about where and how I would wear each outfit, and practicing making the facial expressions the models made in their photos.

The old man who ran the store, and maybe was the owner, would watch me sometimes, but he never said anything. He would just stare at me, the same way he stared at the black kids when they came in to buy records, and make little noises in his throat. I don't know what he was thinking, but I remember always making sure to buy something before I left just in case that curried favor with the guy. Of course, I could not buy the magazines because I could neither bring myself to even imagine throwing them away or imagine how I would explain them if my parents found them in my room. Instead, I would always stop at the cassette racks on the way out, and take the time to find a single or album – depending on how much money I had – to purchase. I figured that as long as I bought a cassette I could potentially ease the stare of the old guy, and I would always have a handy reason for why I went to the store so much.

I took other precautions when I visited the store. Whenever boys who appeared to potentially be my age came into the shop, for example, I would slide over to the sports section right beside the fashion section so it would look like I was looking at baseball or basketball magazines. In fact, I usually sat in between the two sections to make this type of adjustment easier in the moment. I also figured out early on that some of the sports almanac magazines – you know, those old things that covered a certain big event or year in a sport – made great covers for the fashion magazines. I would grab one that looked inconspicuous enough, the special issue on Super Bowl champions throughout the years was a favorite, and then open it to the very middle. Then, I would slide each fashion and women's magazine I wanted to read into the center of the book so I could read it without any potential passerby knowing what I was reading.

I don't remember anyone telling me to do this, but somehow I remember knowing that reading those magazines could be dangerous if the wrong people saw me. Maybe it was the ways boys talked about girls, maybe it was the regular occurrence of the word fag among the same boys, but very early on I got the message that being interested in girly stuff was not something to advertise and, like my love for Jordan, I learned to hide it just in case.

CHAPTER 6

"Shoot the ball you tool," Zach screamed as I dribbled on the edge of the court. Instead of doing so, I passed out to another kid who nailed a three from the corner giving us the game. Laughing and muttering, "Assholes," Zach began gathering his stuff and we started walking toward his house.

"What you homos doing tonight," Zach asked as we turned into our neighborhood.

There it was, another day, another game, another win or loss in the shadow of the private Christian school on the edge of our neighborhood – this was life in the spring following my fourteenth birthday. The school had been founded before any of us could remember, and it offered a combination of Christian life training and rigorous elementary, middle, and high school studies according to its marketing materials. In reality, most of the people in the school either went to the church attached to it or, like Zach, were on the basketball team. Jordan fit neither of these markers. Instead, he went to the school because his mom believed a private education was more likely to save him from her own lower working class fate than a public one.

Unfortunately, being neither a jock nor a church member meant Jordan was basically an automatic outcast at school. It probably did not help matters that he was socially awkward, a little feminine in his interests and mannerisms, and very shy. Not surprisingly, Jordan's perception of the school had little to do with the academics available there. Rather, Jordan hated the place, and pretty much felt like he was constantly under attack throughout every day of his education. Well, every day until Zach arrived.

We met Zach when he moved in to my neighborhood the day after my fourteenth birthday. Zach had a cool persona, as Jordan would say, wherein he seemed to be interested in and aware of every major fashion, sporting, and music trend just before everyone else figured it out. Zach's family members were all in the military, and he planned to enlist as well even though he really seemed to hate his family. At the time, this made little sense to me, but I don't think I ever heard Zach say one positive thing about any of them. Before then, however, he planned to play basketball, smoke pot, and as he was fond of saying, "Nail all the hot Carolina gals he could get his hands on." Since Zach had pretty much every rap cassette available at the time, a fast friendship formed within Zach's first few days in town.

The arrangement was also beneficial for Zach and Jordan. While Zach was about the smoothest kid we ever met, he carried a genuine distaste for the vast majority of other people. Jordan, on the other hand, was incredibly shy and preferred to keep to himself while surrounded by the Christians who populated and controlled his school. This was especially funny to me because Jordan also considered himself a Christian. Whereas church was a chore for Abs and I, Jordan really believed and wanted to be accepted in the faith. The meeting of these two in the same school meant that neither of them would have to be completely alone as they slogged through the final semester of middle school and the entirety of high school. Instead, Zach's status as a jock made Jordan safer in the halls of the school for as long as they remained close friends. At the same time, Jordan was one of the few people Zach did not seem to hate, and as a result, he actually had a friend he enjoyed hanging out with at school. Not surprisingly, the two began to shadow each other, and almost no one messed with either of them in the coming years.

The arrangement was also beneficial for me for different reasons. As I became more and more comfortable with my feminine side and my desire to spend time with girls, Zach provided Jordan with another guy to spend time with who did not much care for the girly side of life aside from his constantly expressed sexual desires. I remember that early on it really bothered me that Zach seemed to care not at all for girls as people, and only saw them as things to collect and discard. I still feel like that would have led me away from spending time with him if I had been in a place where that was not simply the normal way most guys acted. At the time, it bothered me, but I had other things to worry about.

The three of us developed a pattern wherein we would meet after school, play some basketball, make fun of each other, and then head back into the neighborhood. Since the school they attended was both on the northern edge of our neighborhood and on my way home from the school I attended in the nicer neighborhood where Jessica lived, it was a perfect plan that provided a nice release after a long day at school. On the weekends, Zach began accompanying Jordan and I on our adventures, and the two of them often hung out doing "guy stuff" whenever I was busy with Jessica or any of my female friends. At other times, we would all congregate – often with other guys from the basketball team and girls from the school – at Zach's house because he had what was basically his own private home in the basement of the place. We would sit down there for hours hiding from the rest of the world and just being goofy kids. I remember feeling jealous that Zach basically could avoid the prying eyes of anyone else anytime he wanted to by simply locking himself down in that basement where no one could see or hear anything that he might do. All told, this new friendship was a useful arrangement that quickly became normal in our lives, but it did create two problems.

The first problem was that Zach did not do well around girls. Lena, Jessica, Abs, and every other girl I can remember being involved in our lives at the time detested him. All of them agreed that he was attractive with his soft auburn hair, smooth smile, and tanned, muscular body, but all of them equally agreed he was about the most annoying person they had ever met. This problem arose primarily because Zach did not know how to talk to girls without attempting to find a way into their panties. He would constantly hit on them or make sexual jokes. They, in turn, would grow tired of turning him down, and hearing never ending sexual jokes at their expense. As a result, Zach would usually only last a few minutes to a half an hour after any female emerged, which drastically limited my time with him and whenever Jordan left with him, limited my time with Jordan.

The second problem arose whenever girls were not around. Zach basically wanted to hang out with the guys – Jordan, me, or both of us – all the time. This, however, made it very difficult for Jordan and I to spend time alone, and was further complicated by the fact that we were fairly sure it would not be smart to let Zach know about all of our relationship. Like most of the guys we grew up with, Zach fairly regularly made comments about fags and homos during basketball games and other interactions. The problem, of course, was that we could never tell whether or not such comments were the result of normal ways of talking taught in our community, or signals that we would be in danger if the person speaking knew we loved each other in a more-than-friends way. We thus did not show or discuss our romantic relationship with Zach just to be safe, which meant that anytime we spent with Zach required us to pretend to be just another couple of guy friends.

At first, Jordan and I argued about these problems. Jordan wanted to hang out with Zach because being alone at that school with no friends had been torture for as long as he could remember, and because the two of them had a lot of common interests. Simply put, he really liked the guy, and wrote off his more erratic or annoying characteristics as no big deal. I did not feel the same way because I felt like Zach was being a jerk to my other friends and getting in the way of my time with Jordan. My arguments were mostly selfish, I admit, but they felt important to me. In the end, I conceded that thanks to the girls I had no clue what it was like to feel alone at school – a Christian school at that. I backed off, and we kept hanging out with Zach despite my concerns. I figured that I could handle the things about him I didn't like for the sake of Jordan, and I kind of just got used to how he acted and so did the girls. Over time, we just didn't really notice the annoying stuff as Zach became more of a fixture in our little group of misfits.

"Nothing much," Jordan and I both said at about the same time.

Zach reached into his book bag, and motioned for us to come closer. Inside, he had a bottle labeled Jack Daniels. Neither Jordan nor I had been exposed much to liquor at this point, but we both knew what it was. Licking his lips, Zach asked, "So y'all wanna grab a drink? I swiped it from the old man, and my folks are out at the base until late tonight, what you think?" I thought it was likely a waste of a good evening, but I was pretty sure Jordan had other thoughts on the subject. I had also just spent the last two nights at Zach's place, and I needed a break.

Laughing, I say, "No way for me man – Abs and I got into some of that a couple weeks ago and I ended up sick as a dog." This was true, but I really just did not feel like a Zach night at that moment, and kind of wanted to go home.

"Damn, that's messed up, but Abs sure is hot – you get in that man?"

Shaking my head and wondering if Zach ever thinks of anything else, I say, "Nope, and likely never will, Abs and I don't see each other like that. She's like a sister to me."

Laughing, Zach says, "More for me," and smacks Jordan on the back before adding, "You should tell her to hook me up sometime." I didn't know why, but smacking people on the back seemed to be the only kind of physical contact Zach was comfortable with around us. He would wince when Jordan or I hugged each other or another guy goodbye, but smacking the shit out of each other seemed to be his way of showing affection. At this point, we approached Zach's place, and he turned to Jordan saying, "So you out too, or you want to get good?"

Looking at me, then at Zach, then back at me, Jordan shrugs and says, "My mom ain't going to be home until late so what the hell mate, let's have a party."

"That's right," Zach says lighting a cigarette and handing one to Jordan. He lights Jordan's smoke, and turns to me, "You gonna stay and hang man?"

"Nah, I think I'll head home. Y'all have a good time."

Looking at me as I start to leave, Jordan asks, "You okay?"

Before I respond, Zach blows out smoke and says, "Yeah, she's good, she just don't feel like partying tonight, right baby?" He was always saying shit like that to me, and it was funny because I was both offended by the fact that I knew he meant it as an insult even if only in fun, and delighted that someone was referring to me as a girl. For me, Zach always seemed to be full of these types of contradictions.

Laughing along with Zach, I respond, "Yep, that's it Zach" as I walk down the hill toward my house.

CHAPTER 7

"What's new sweetheart," Abs asks as she comes bouncing down the path that leads from the abandoned railroad tracks to the river. The railroad tracks run primarily south to north and vice versa from the nicer end of town where Jessica lives to the little downtown area somewhat south of the park. They are situated along the river, and hug the park where Jordan and I generally meet. The woods on each side of the tracks provide endless playgrounds for teenagers in need of privacy. As Abs comes closer, I notice the sounds of the water rushing through the rocks are calming, steady, and sweet to my ears while I sit on the bank staring up at her.

"Well, Zach wants to have sex with you," I say with a smile, and she starts laughing the deep, throaty laugh she has had for as long as I've known her.

Abigail – or Abs – and I met in elementary school. We were assigned to be cubbyhole buddies in kindergarten, and in some ways we retain this status. Abs was always at least as strange as I was, and we would spend hours just talking about our favorite pop stars – I loved Madonna, she loved Janet Jackson, we idolized both – and laughing at life. A curvy blonde with glasses, freckles that slowly dissipated as the years went by, and a throaty laugh, Abs remains the definition of fun in my mind all these years later. She had a way of cutting through all the fear, sadness, and bad shit of any situation, and just celebrating every moment whether she was writing cartoon inspired poetry on your arm or dancing with reckless abandonment and very little skill in the middle of a playground. Whether or not anyone else was, Abs was truly alive.

When she finishes laughing, she says, "Well doesn't Zach want to have sex with everyone? I mean, come on, Zach would screw a tree if you put tits on it and told him it was called Molly." She starts laughing again, and so do I. "I mean, I'm not sure if I should feel flattered or go home and bathe repeatedly for the next three days." We continue to laugh, and she takes a seat beside me carefully settling her Winnie the Pooh purse in the dirt.

"He asked me to put in a word for him, so you know, a word," I say and we both start laughing again.

"You know, I feel like he will either become amazing at it, or be the biggest regret so many girls have just because of how cocky he already is." She pulls a pack of smokes out of her bag, and offers me one. She knows I won't take it, and I know she knows that, but she always offers anyhow. It seems like everyone other than Jessica and her friends smokes these days. I wonder when that happened. "Who knows, maybe I'll try him out one day just to see."

At this, we both start laughing again, and she almost chokes on her cigarette. After the laughter dissipates, we sit in silence for a few minutes tossing rocks into the river. We have a lot of these silences in our relationship. Oftentimes, we both just have nothing to say, but somehow, we also both know that the other one is okay with that and will wait if necessary. She smokes her cigarette, I sip my soda, and we watch the river for a few minutes. The water rushes by as if in a hurry, but of course, it really has nowhere to go. Something about it is mesmerizing. We often come to this spot – just about 200 yards from the ledge hanging over the river where the older kids put up the swing that falls down every few years and get drunk and stoned each summer. The spot is comfortable, and peaceful, but most importantly, it is a space we have shared many conversations throughout our young lives.

"Anything else interesting this week, you know, other than my new lover," she asks while opening her own soda can. I've never known anyone else who opened soda – or later beer – cans the way Abs does. Instead of using the tab, she always used her pocketknife, which never seemed to leave her side, to cut a hole in the top of the can. She would then smooth out the edges of the can, kind of sand them down, and just drink out of the little hole she made. She does this now, and as usual, I marvel at her creativity.

"What do you do when you like two people?"

"Ooh, tasty, Jessica is not enough for you?" She tips the ash from her cigarette, moves a piece of strawberry blonde hair out of her face, and continues, "I think it depends on the people. You know, you try to figure out who you like more, and go with that and if you're not me it might work out for you." We both laugh for a moment at her, thus far, terrible luck with guys. She inspires damn near every boy she meets, and they fall head over heels for her, but without doubt, at some point they turn into creeps and must be, as she always says, taken out to where the trash lives. "I had this issue with Josh and Mike last fall. I really loved Mike's jokes, his ability to spend money on me, and his lips when we kissed, but Josh was just so yummy and I kept thinking he should be mine, you know, like all mine in every way. And, you know, I left Mike for Josh, and it was fun at first, you know, but then he got really boring – I mean, a cute butt only gets you so far sweetie – and Mike was already seeing that annoying Becca girl so, you know, you choose and maybe it will work out."

At this moment, I come the closest I ever have to telling Abs about Jordan, but I just can't do it. Not yet, not now. I choke the information back down, and think maybe someday I'll tell her. It actually bothers me that she doesn't know. I don't like keeping anything from Abs, and I will never find a way to make doing so feel okay. Instead, I say, "Well, how do you tell which one you like more? I mean, can you like two people the same or in different ways?"

Smiling, she says, "Of course you can, but they probably won't like that. Who is the second fiddle trying to steal you from sweet, innocent little Jessica? You think you got a real shot with Lena maybe?" Abs does not like Jessica, or Becca, or any of the good kids from the nicer neighborhood, and like me, she kind of grew up in Lena's shadow and embrace. She thinks the good kids are all a bunch of spoiled assholes, and will happily celebrate the ones who end up with shitty lives in later years. She thinks I should look to "our" people instead.

I lie. "Oh, its just a girl I met at the park that seems really sweet and I don't know, I adore Jessica, but I wonder why I can't be with both of them." Truthfully, there is no doubt that if I had to choose I would choose Jordan, but my response needs to fit the either or idea she proposed, and I don't want to have to make up details about the girl from the park. I often find myself in these situations where I have to adjust my answers to fit the preconceived ideas of other people, and I wonder if it will always be this way.

"Oh sweetie, that's probably just a crush, you should ignore that. I know it sounds funny, but you're going to always see more girls you like, and you can't just chase them all. You have to appreciate what you have with Jessica unless there is some problem."

"No, there is no problem with Jessica."

"Then stay with Jessica, and just let the crush go."

I nod knowing that she intends to help and knowing as well that this is no help at all. I love Jordan, but I also think I might love Jessica and I don't know how to choose between them because I can be open with Jessica but Jordan and I have to hide things. I don't know what to do so I simply ask, "What about you, anything new?"

Abs and I always have these catch up sessions because in school and at church we don't really talk to each other much anymore. Luckily, the silence is a phase that will soon come to an end. I don't really know or understand why we stopped talking in public, but she says I cramp her style. We used to hang out all the time no matter where we were, but sometime in sixth grade a rumor started that we were dating and Abs said that all the other boys stopped talking to her. This doesn't really make sense to me, but it bothered her a lot at the time. She was so mad at me, but I didn't do anything and I pointed that out…three months later when she started talking to me again. Since then, we don't hang out as much in public places though we still do at times, but either way, we still talk almost every day and meet in private to discuss whatever is going on in our lives. Well, whatever is going on in our lives that does not include my attraction to other boys or my desire to dress like girls that is.

"Yes, actually, I'm going to have sex." I just stare at her for a minute, and she laughs, "Don't look at me like that, I haven't been hiding anyone from you. I don't know who it will be, but I know I want to have sex now, I'm ready." Oh, that made more sense. I did wonder what I missed, but I could not really say anything since she did not know about parts of my life. In any case, I remembered how nervous and scared she got last summer when Darryl – the great summer kisser as she called him – asked about sex so I figured I should ask a few questions.

"Are you sure you're ready?"

"Yes, I have been thinking about it all year, and I think its time. I mean, come on, even you have already done it," she said and lit another cigarette. Abs found out about Lena and I when Lena decided to tell her, and suggest that we would make a fun couple. I then filled her in on the details, well most of the details. I didn't tell her about the closet, or my interest in dressing like Lena, but I told her about the sex and about the next week when we did other stuff and the week after that. "But no, I know you were scared last summer when I was so upset, but I'm really ready now and I think it will be good for me."

"Is there any way I can help you or be there for you?"

Abs and I were often each other's support systems, and if she was sure, my only real thought was about ways I could be a good friend to her in this latest experience. We had already been through so many major life moments. She was there when I damn near died learning to ride a bike, and I witnessed her own near suicide with the same lesson. She was there when we first had real tests in schools, and when we navigated the transition to middle school. I was there when her parents looked like they might divorce, and when some jerk called her fat and she responded by kicking the crap out of him and got suspended from school for two weeks. I was there when her two older friends got raped at different times at different parties, and we tried to figure out how something like that could happen in the first place and what we could do to protect ourselves when we started going to parties. If either of us had a rock we could lean on at any time, it was each other, and I was ready to do what I could as she explored this latest transition the same way I held her when she got freaked out the year before about sex.

"Well, do you know anything about sex, I mean, other than what Lena has taught us?"

The sad part is the answer to this question was a resounding no. We lived in South Carolina. We went to public school in a very conservative, Christian area. We had no sex education. All we really knew was that sex was apparently deadly, evil, and would make baby Jesus cry. We barely had any clue about relationships in general, and sex was pretty much never mentioned except when some adult was talking about how evil it was. I knew nothing beyond what Lena taught me. Oh Lena, without her we would have been even more clueless than we were throughout our teen years. She was our sex education.

"Nope, I got some things out of the magazines at the store, but nothing helpful really. Well, wait, I did read an article on condoms and copied the diagrams for how to use them right. Wait a minute," I said as I started rummaging in my bag, "Here you go," I said handing her the sheet of handwritten notes. I spent a couple hours in the store copying these from a magazine on a day when the owner was distracted by an older guy named Roger who came in with questions about collectible sets of jewelry. Jordan actually knew Roger from his days hanging out at the diner his mom used to work at, and we both kind of looked up to the guy because he openly loved another man named Daniel. While the owner was busy excitedly discussing the collections with Roger, I copied and made notes on an article that showed the reasons for and ways to use condoms that, it said, everyone should know.

She lights another smoke, and says, "Yeah, I should probably use those. Do you know a good place to get them?"

"Well, the bait shop probably has them, and since they sell y'all cigarettes and wine and stuff I'm sure they won't care, but you could just go to Lena, she has a ton of them." The bait shop was on the main road before you got to the magazine shop. It was just this little run down shop that looked like it might have once been a gas station, and also looked like it was out of business most of the time. The owner was a funny old man who did not believe, as he said, in age restrictions for the good stuff, and it was probably the gang of teens going in every week for cigarettes and beer and other illicit goods that kept the place open. Other than Lena, the bait shop was the ultimate source of illicit materials for kids in our neighborhood.

"A ton?"

"Yeah, her mom gave her a big bag of them when she turned fourteen, and just keeps giving her more every few months. I guess her mom thinks she should be having more sex than she is or something because she basically has a whole drawer full of condoms now. That's where I got one to try out the tips in the article." I actually got a few, but then I got scared my parents would find them and threw away all the ones that I had not opened to test the tips in the article. With Lena about to move, I made a mental note to get some more, and find a place to hide them at my house.

I asked her about condoms the second time we had intercourse. I had just read the article about the things, and I wondered why we didn't use them. She showed me her collection, but said that she didn't see any reason for them because she had some kind of pill, and neither of us likely had any of the health stuff. She explained that she always used them with people she was dating at first, but that most guys didn't like them for some reason. Years later, when Lena was in college, we would laugh and despair at just how naïve we were about safe sex.

Laughing and choking on her smoke a bit, she says, "Well, hell, that is much easier than buying them."

"So, do you have a plan or anything?"

"Not really, I mean, I know it won't be with Simon."

Wondering why the boy she was currently dating was disqualified, I had to ask, "Why not?"

"Well, Simon is amazing and I think I might even love him, but…" and for a minute she just kind of stares at the ground, "Well, his thing is huge and that's a little intimidating for a first try."

I can't help it. I bust out laughing and spill my soda down the ledge in the process before composing myself somewhat and saying, "Yeah, I could see that."

Punching me in the arm, she says, "Shut up, that thing might not even fit in me! I mean, you know, he might be where the rumor about black boy's things got started, it's like a pole, I'm not even kidding. What the hell am I supposed to do with that? " Now, we're both laughing, and she adds, "And, you know, I really like Simon so I don't know, I feel like our first time should be special, and that is not what I expect from what I've heard about other people's first times. I think you have to work up to it, you know, the special stuff." I nod thinking about the storeroom and the wine that was not really wine. "So, I don't know, I'm thinking about Mark actually because Simon will be gone all summer and Mark will be home visiting."

"Mark? Tammy's big brother?"

"Yeah, I mean, he's older, he's experienced, and he has a really pretty you know."

"Wait, you've seen Mark's thing," I gasp trying to hide my desire to see it too. Mark is utterly beautiful, and I'm pretty sure everyone in the neighborhood – boys and girls alike – has thought about his body in ways that make baby Jesus cry.

"Yeah, a couple years ago Lindsey's parents were out of town for the weekend so I stayed over, and that was when Lindsey's sister was dating Mark and one morning, Mark just walked out of the bedroom naked and we both saw it."

Laughing, I say, "That must have been a fun morning."

Laughing too, she adds, "It sure woke me up," before falling to the side holding her ribs as we both slip into uncontrollable giggles. After a few minutes, she asks, "So, what about you hotshot, are you going to do it with Jessica?"

"I don't know," I say and that is actually the truth. On the one hand, I want to have sex with Jessica, but Jessica is not sure if she's ready for that. On the other hand, I don't want to do it with Jessica because I'm worried it will upset Jordan the same way my experiences with Lena have upset him. I really just do not know what I would do if Jessica gave me the opportunity.

"I think you should, you two are too cute."

"I'm sure I'll take your opinion into consideration when the time comes."

"Of course you will, I'm brilliant."

And with that, we slide into another peaceful silence as the river runs along its track. I don't know what Abs is thinking about, but all I can think about is Jordan and Jessica, and what in the world you're supposed to do when you fall for two people before you have any clue about relationships.

CHAPTER 8

One night near the end of spring, Jordan doesn't show up at the park. I'm standing in our usual meeting spot in the grass where we first kissed, but there is no sign of him. Where the hell is he, I wonder while continuously scanning the surrounding areas.

Jordan and I realized even as eight and eight-and-a-half-year-olds that two boys kissing in the grass would not be met with welcome in our little town. We admitted right away that we liked each other. We agreed right away that there was nothing wrong with that despite what both our churches seemed to think. We also agreed right away that it had to be our little secret. We worked out a plan where we would meet at the park in this spot, our spot, and then disappear into the woods taking every possible precaution along the way. Each meeting would be set up verbally – in person or on the phone only after making sure no one else was on the line – with no evidence left behind for the wrong eyes to see. We were young, we were in love, but we weren't stupid, and we had already heard horror stories about what could happen to boys like us. We didn't want to know what that would feel like.

We were ten years old or so when Jordan told me he had always liked boys. He had never seen a girl he liked, and figured if there ever was one he would consider it then. I told him I had always liked boys and girls. I also told him that I thought I might be a girl or like to dress like one sometimes. He also told me he had health problems since he was little, but no one had ever told him what they were or why he had them. I also told him that I liked girl clothes, singers, and games more than boy stuff a lot of the time, but when I told people that they were often mean to me so I learned how to keep quiet. He also told me that he constantly wondered who and where his dad was, and often got angry just thinking about it. We told each other everything from the start, and we both felt somehow more free having someone who really seemed to understand and accept us as we were.

Keeping with this tradition, I told him about what Lena and I did when I met up with him that night in the park. He wasn't happy about it, but he listened. He thought it was good that I did it first with

Lena instead of some what's his or her name again, and wanted to know if I was going to do it again. I said I didn't know. He asked me, for the first time since before he went to camp the year before, if I wanted to do it with him. I told him I did, but I understood why he did not want to. He reiterated that he was scared to do it with me. He was scared to do it again at all. He again talked about how hard it already was not to be able to tell anyone about me, his "friend," and how he thought it would only get worse if we did that. I reiterated that I understood and I again talked about how we did not have to with each other and that I would not with anyone else if he asked. He agreed he would not with anyone else if I asked.

Once again that night, neither of us asked.

The park is very cold tonight, and very quiet. There are no games tonight. Some of the lights are on, and it is nice to be out in the night. Abs is ready and waiting if my parents try to find me even though she doesn't know where I really am. She probably thinks I'm meeting Jessica, but she never asks. I love that about Abs.

Jordan is thirty minutes late. Jordan is never late.

Jordan's mom works the middle shift today so she will be home soon. She works at a gas station on the other side of town, and picks up some season work and extra shifts at a local diner. When Jordan was little, his mom would take him to work with her and he would mingle with the people. It was in that diner where he first met Roger, the older man who shared his life with another man. Roger would tell Jordan stories about the good ole days, and about his husband. Jordan's mom would remind Jordan that they weren't really married every time. Jordan looked up to Roger, and always dreamed of a life like the one Roger described. Jordan's mom doesn't know this, and in a few years when she finds out, she will not react well.

It was also in that diner that Jordan met his first real friend. She was some girl that he said was kind of like Roger's daughter, but she didn't live with Roger. What was her name, I wondered sitting in the park thinking about the past. Anyway, she had moved away when her mom got another job, and Jordan missed her a lot. This happened not long after we met, and I kind of became his only source of friendship – alongside time he spent with Lena and Abs whenever they came around – until we met Zach. I wondered what it felt like to be so alone. I was barely social at all compared to most of the kids we knew, but at least I had a couple people to talk to. He never said anything about it, but I think the loneliness really bothered him a lot.

I'm standing by the edge of the woods when I realize Jordan is almost an hour late. We always meet by the edge of the woods because kids go play in the woods and no one is suspicious of two boys going to play in the woods. Behind the park, there is an old abandoned railroad track that we all call the path, the same one that runs along the river from south to north, which goes from downtown – what little downtown we have – all the way through part of the town, behind neighborhoods like mine and Jordan's, all the way to the other side of town where the nicer houses and the good kids live. We usually walk the path to a certain tree, and then slip into the woods to be alone. Our tree is not by any of the established foot paths kids use to get to the river, to get to the stream area where people do drugs, or to get in and out of the neighborhoods. Instead, we created a path of our own with rocks and other small signals that – we hope – no one else will ever notice. I doubt even Abs could find it with her superhuman sight. Back there, down our path that we make sure doesn't become an obvious path, in the woods, we can be free for a few minutes or hours at a time.

When Jordan is just past an hour late, I begin walking toward his house. I am scared something has happened to him along the way. I remember Leonard, another man from the diner years ago. Leonard was assaulted walking through Jordan's neighborhood one night by another person who apparently needed money and was never caught. What if something like that has happened? What if something worse has happened? Where the hell is he?

I start feeling myself tremble with fear. I am scared one of the groups of kids that yell fag at everyone has decided to do more than yell. I am scared he is still mad at me for having sex with Lena a few times or even more mad than he seemed when we talked about it each time it happened. Maybe he is done with me and doesn't think I'm worth being told this fact. I am pissed off at him for scaring me. More than anything though, I just really want to see him tonight – I want to feel his arms around me, hear his voice, and just feel that rush for a little bit before I have to go back to the real world again. I just want to know he's okay.

I walk through the fields that people play sports on, that we played sports on as kids, and I cross the park's main road. I cut through the smaller section of woods on Jordan's side of the park, hop the creek that will one day have a little bridge but does not yet, and find myself in his neighborhood. The houses here are smaller than the ones on my side of the park, the same way the ones on my side of the park are smaller than the ones where Jessica lives, and the same way the ones where Jessica lives are still smaller than the ones out near the country club on the edge of town. I think about one of the guys that works with Jordan's mom. A creepy sort of fella named Roy who is always making passes at Jordan's mom. What if Jordan's mom is hurt? What if Jordan and Roy finally did get in a fight? I'm scared, so I keep walking.

As I walk, I keep playing with a little pink headband Jordan got me at camp. He said it could be my girly uniform, like my own pink batsuit or superman cape that I could hide from other people and pull out when I really need to feel like a girl. What if something happened to him? I twist the little pink band in my hand and think about the first time we kissed, the first time we danced, the first time he said he loved me. I think about the way the world gets brighter when he smiles at me. I think about walking by the edge of the river with him – a little distance between us just in case – watching the sun set and the world go quiet the way it always does. What if he fell on the way to meet me, maybe he took a different path than this one and I missed him, what if he's hurting in the dark? He could be all alone, unconscious, bleeding, I don't know, he could be…

…SITTING ON HIS FUCKING FRONT PORCH. I can't help it, I scream at him, "What are you doing? Do you know how worried I was? You asshole!" I've never been much of a screamer, never all that loud in general, but Jordan often pulls the volume out of me in some way. A few years later, Abs says its something about emotions. I feel consumed by rage. I want to kick his perfect little ass! How dare he scare me like that? How dare he make me worry? He could have been hurt, he could have been killed, he could have been in real trouble, but no, he is sitting on his damn porch standing me up. What an asshole!

He doesn't answer, jerk! I finally get close enough to hit him, and then I see it – he's crying. I can't explain it to this day, but every ounce of anger I have falls away, and I reach out for him. "What's wrong," I say as I close in on him, "Are you hurt?"

He looks up at me from the porch, and in a broken voice says, "I'm sorry I didn't make it to the park."

"Forget the park, you're crying, what is going on?"

He looks behind him to make sure his mom is out of sight, reaches for my hand, and in that same broken voice says, "Somebody killed Daniel," and I can't breathe, I can't see, the whole world suddenly seems dark.

CHAPTER 9

Jordan's mom came home right as he was heading out to meet me. She was exhausted. Her co-worker drove her home because she was a mess. She poured a drink, took a couple of her sleeping pills, and told Jordan she was going to bed. Worried, Jordan asked her what happened, and she just said talk to Linda before slamming her bedroom door. Jordan hated Linda and was sure the feeling was mutual, but he wanted to know what was going on and why his mom looked like she was ready to die.

Standing in the doorway, Linda said, "Don't worry Jordan, your mom will be fine. She just had a hell of a night at work."

"What happened," he asked feeling even more worried.

"Did you ever meet that old fairy that used to come to the diner when your mom worked over yonder? What was his name, Robby, Raymond, something like that? Well, anyhoo, his friend comes by the store pretty regularly to get some of that gay stuff, you know, condoms and what not, and drinks. Well, I don't know for sure what all happened, but tonight he ran into some boys in the parking lot and they got upset with him, don't know why, maybe he said something funny, you know, maybe he touched 'em or something who knows how those people are, and they beat him mercilessly right there in front of your poor mama's little window, right there in front of her like that. Isn't that terrible, she saw the whole thing! Oh my sweet Jesus, to have to see something so ugly, I just can't imagine."

Trembling inside, wanting to scream, thinking his name was Roger not old fairy and that was his husband not some friend dammit, Jordan stood there staring at Linda at a loss for words.

"And that ain't even the worst of it honey. For some reason, the guy tried to fight back, it was probably funny him trying to fight like a man, oh sweet Jesus, anyhoo, he tried to fight back the cops said, and hit one of them little boys with one of the beers in his bag. Well, you know what, sure enough, that just made them angrier, and the one that got hit, kind of like the ringleader of the group the cop guessed, you know how that goes, well just, you know, he just hauled off and slammed a tire iron against the old guy's head and there was blood everywhere, even when I got there you could still see the mess. It was such a dreadful mess, they are gonna have to hose that off good I tell you, whoo, it was a scene."

Overcome, Jordan collapsed onto the couch.

"I know honey, I know, such a horrible thing for your mama. She's gonna need our support is all, it'll be alright I promise you. Terrible that she had to see all that, but she gonna be okay, I promise you, she'll be fine, just a little rattled and such."

Slowly, Jordan asked, "What…happened…to…the…guy?"

"Oh honey, you don't need to worry about him, he's gone to meet Jesus now or wherever people like that go when they pass, bless his heart, he got into a fight with the wrong boys is what he did. Yep, that's what he did, whatever he said to them or what not, he got in the wrong fight is what he did, I tell you, probably should be more careful is what I say, but you know how they are, all in your face and such, just got in the wrong fight is all. It's just so sad, you know, first you get afflicted with that stuff like, I mean, bless their hearts, it must be terrible to have that type of thing in you, terrible I say, but that and then you end up meeting your maker in a parking lot. It's just sad is what it is, I don't see why…"

Jordan couldn't remember what else she said. All he could think about was Roger. His husband was dead, killed by some punk kids for no reason. Killed. Dead. In a parking lot, all alone, away from Roger, all alone, dead. Jordan couldn't wrap his head around it. Everything seemed loud and quiet all at the same time. How could someone just… is that what we had to look forward to…what would Roger do now.

As we sat there on the porch that night, I realized Jordan did not remember coming outside. I wanted to tell him something to make it all better. I wanted to tell myself something to make it all better. I wanted to pretend to be strong. I wanted to say we could fight them together. I wanted to say things would be different someday. I wanted to believe things would be better someday or maybe somewhere else. I wanted to do or say something that mattered, that helped, that could ease the pain we both felt in that moment. I wanted so many things as we both sat there shaking on the front porch, but all I could do was hold Jordan tighter and hope we would feel better in the morning.

The walk home that night felt ten times as long as normal. I swore I saw people wielding tire irons and screaming at me from behind every bush and tree. I imagined the music director coming into the storeroom wielding a tire iron with a picture of baby Jesus on it. I imagined a lot of things, all of them terrifying. I wondered what Jordan was doing, would he be able to sleep, and what his mom might say in the morning. I didn't stop by Abs' house and knock on her window like I normally did. I didn't really care if I got in trouble that night. I didn't really know how to care about anything as I walked through the quiet neighborhood past a bunch of menacing tire iron wielding bushes and shrubs.

There was only a small mention of Daniel in the paper in the morning. There was a story about a fight that turned deadly at the store, but there were no details about the victim – his name, his hobbies, his sexuality, his loved ones, none of that was mentioned. I checked the next day's paper too, nothing. I checked the next paper and the next, still nothing. It was like he disappeared in the parking lot that night, forgotten by the town he lived in for most of his life. There were also no details on the assailants in any of the papers. Who were they? Did they get caught? Were they still out there somewhere just waiting for the next one of us to become visible? I didn't know, but I thought about it every day for years to come.

CHAPTER 10

The last week of school I went to stay with my grandmother. I was happy to be excused from class, and my parents were happy to have someone there full time since my grandmother had been having health issues. I honestly had no clue what I might do while I was there to keep from dying of boredom, but I embraced the new scenery and the chance to miss some school without having to worry about getting in trouble.

Little did I know, this would actually turn out to be one of the nicest things my parents ever did for me.

On my second day there, I became curious about the room in the back of the house that I had never seen anyone go in before, and I wondered what could be behind that door. When my grandmother went down for her afternoon nap, I decided to find out for myself. I was feeling pretty down in the weeks following Daniel's death, and I felt like if I could just find something to distract me from the lack of communication from Jordan and the sadness of what happened I would feel at least a little bit better. I took the key my grandmother left on the kitchen table, and walked into a magical world.

Inside the door, strewn about all over the room, was a collection of ladies' clothing that could rival a department store. I think the feeling I experienced staring at the piles of blouses, skirts, dresses, and accessories could best be described as orgasmic. I spent the two hours I had that day simply looking through all the different options, and trying to decide if I was actually awake or simply having this dream for about the billionth time. By the time I accepted the room was actually real, however, my grandmother's afternoon medicine alarm started going off and I was out of time.

I replaced the key, and looked after my grandmother for the rest of the day like I had the day before, but all I could think about was the room. Of course, my grandmother would decide to stay up even later than usual that night watching her stories, and I felt like every minute took at least an hour to pass. In the end, she finally went to sleep. Key in hand, I went back to the room, and the adventure began.

I started with a green silk blouse, a set of pearls, and a soft black skirt. I put on the clothes, feeling stronger and happier with each piece, and did my own modeling show for the mirror. I giggled like a child, and then I found an old dress like something out of a 1950s movie that I paired with a cute pair of strappy shoes. I posed for the cameras and explained how much I appreciated the attention of the fans. As I was accepting yet another award, a lovely sweater set with diamond patterning caught my eyes. I put on the sweater set – with matching skirt of course – and sat on the bed looking at the door. Softly, I whispered, "Yes Jordan, come and take me away my love," and blew kisses at the door.

Variations of this ritual continued over the next four nights. Each day, during my grandmother's afternoon nap, I would line up a series of outfits in the room. Then, after she went to sleep each night, I would stay up for hours trying on the clothes, trying out different lives, and having the most exquisite imaginary dates with Jessica and Jordan. Lena and I even went out a few times, and Abs and I starred in a fashion show in New York one night in that room. Sometimes I went to the new fancy restaurant in town with Jessica and Jordan, and other times I went out with only one or the other, but every time I was dressed to kill and looking hot. It was a kind of heaven built especially for me, and I wished it would never end.

During the rest of my time at my grandmother's, everything was normal. We talked about the old days, and how her and her friends were some of the first female workers in the mills. She told me about how they fought with supervisors, escaped abusive husbands, and cheered the activists who made it possible for women to have more in this country. We listened to her old Judds records, drank coffee, and talked about the ways the world changed in her long lifetime. It was just a normal visit for us – she didn't say anything about her failing health and I didn't say anything about the treasure chest I found in the back of the house.

On Sunday morning, my mom arrived with the new nurse who would be taking care of my grandmother. I felt an illogical desire to break this nurse's hip so I could keep playing with my clothes, but instead I spoke with her about the daily routine and thanked her when she complimented me on the care I had given my grandmother. After a while, she went into the living room with my mom to discuss details related to the house and my grandmother's medicine. At the same time, my grandmother asked me to help her out to the front porch, and together we stepped outside.

My grandmother turned to me after I closed the door, and said, "You know, good people come in many different forms little one."

As I often did when she offered advice, I said, "Yes mam," without thinking too much about what she actually said.

"One thing I've learned is that this world is full of people, many of them weak men mind you, who will try to tear you down and make you feel bad. You better not ever let them do that to you. You're one of the good ones, and don't you forget it."

At this point, I started to pay attention. "I won't grandma," I said wondering where she was going with this.

"Another thing I have learned is that nobody thinks nothing when old people lose things, you hear me?" I nodded, and she said, "So I'm going to lose this here key in your hand and if anyone notices I'll get your mama to get me another one just like it." With that, she placed the key to the back room into my hand, and started heading for the door. Just as she started to open it, she turned to me and said, "And be a good boy and get my cigarettes from my bedside table, and while you're at it, you should get rid of the magazine on the table for me, silly articles about how to easily remove makeup and accessorize outfits, what am I going to do with that at my age. You can get rid of that for me can't you little one?"

She didn't wait for me to respond. She just smiled, and went back inside. I stood there turning the key over in my hand and trying not to cry. I didn't know what else to do so I went inside, went to her bedroom, grabbed her cigarettes, and picked up the magazine. The magazine had some pages folded down and marked that provided tips on makeup use, matching women's outfits, and accessories. I put the magazine in my bag, and took her the cigarettes. As she lit one, she grabbed my mom's arm and said, "You know, I think it would be good for me if little one comes to see me from time to time. I like playing cards with him, and I like him to read my magazines to me sometimes.

It's good for him to read to me, and I bet there are a lot of things he could learn from me yet."

As my mom nodded, my grandmother looked right through me and smiled one of the sweetest smiles I have ever seen. Watching the two of them – one being sneaky and the other obviously confused – I just played with my new key in my pocket and thought about the next time I would be in that back room. I also thought about the fact that I now had a perfect excuse for any women's magazines my parents might find in my bedroom.

CHAPTER 11

Summertime came as middle school ended. Down at the basketball court in front of the church where Zach and Jordan went to school a congregation of us would meet almost daily to listen to music and shoot hoops.

A few weeks into the summer, a group of us were shooting hoops when Zach announced that his cousin was coming to town with a driver's license and would trade a ride out to the lake for gas money. Standing in the Carolina heat on yet another miserable June afternoon, this sounded like paradise to all of us. "Just meet down here tomorrow at noon with some cash if you want to go, and we'll head out to the camping area out on the lake to find us some chicks," Zach said between points.

The next day, two trucks were waiting in the parking lot beside Zach. His cousin was driving a Chevy S-10 that looked like it might not have much life left in it, and some other guy was there with an old Ford F-150 that did not look much better. None of this mattered to Jordan, Abs, Lindsey, or me as we sweated our way to the trucks in the middle of the day. Jordan especially was just finally starting to come out into the world again, and unlikely to be deterred by anything short of another death. When we all met at the park, he said, "I never want to see my house again, please let's get the hell out of here," and all of us kind of shared that sentiment. Lindsey lived a few houses down from Jordan, and her house did not have air conditioning, so she was especially interested in anything that involved a break from the heat and cold water.

Zach's cousin, maybe the only family member that he didn't hate, was a guy named Brian who looked like every mechanic you have ever seen in a low budget movie. He had beer or something stained all over a pair of coveralls, and grease stains on his fingers. He was smoking a Lucky Strike and rubbing his crotch when we walked up. His friend was a guy he just called Lucky who looked like he had been unlucky in a handful of bar room brawls over the years. Once again, none of this mattered to the rest of us as we sought sanctuary from the heat that day. We happily met these less than safe looking strangers who were visiting from "Somewhere up in the country near ole Greenville," and gladly jumped into their cars to be taken away to god knows where.

After giving the goons our money, we all got situated in the trucks. Lindsey rode up front with Lucky in his truck, and Jordan and I rode in the back. We wanted some time together even if we would have to be discreet with the others nearby. Abs and Zach shared the front cab of the S-10 with Brian after Zach basically begged Abs to ride with him. Together, our rag tag band of soon to be high schoolers paired with two dirty older looking guys headed out of town. In the back of the F-150, Jordan said, "I'm sorry I've been so quiet lately. I just felt broken after that night." I told him it was cool, and then told him about my adventures at my grandmother's house. "She gave you the key, how did she know?"

"I have no clue, but I guess she doesn't see anything wrong with it."

"Wow, that is so cool."

"I know."

In the front of the F-150, Lindsey was actually having a good time with Lucky. She would tell us later that he was really funny and sweet. We didn't see it, but then again, who knows? Up ahead, the S-10 apparently became a party almost immediately with the three of them passing around a joint and sipping beers as they sang along to a Charlie Daniels tape that was stuck in the stereo of the truck after some undisclosed mishap years prior. According to Abs, Zach would get a bit less annoying with every single swig from his beer can and tug of the joint. Truth be told, he was actually much less annoying to all of us by the time we got to the lake, and I can only guess the substances played a major role in that transformation.

From our neighborhood, it was about a 45-minute drive out to the part of the lake we were going to that day. Basically, all you had to do was head west in the opposite direction of the interstate, and then just keep going until you got to the old bait and tackle shop. The shop itself sold very little bait or tackle, but rather was another shop that teens likely kept in business via illicit sales of beer, cigarettes, and other unsavory items that we were not yet supposed to buy. Once you got to the shop, you took a left turn and continued on until you hit the entrance to the swimming areas nestled off the road between a couple old gas stations. By old, I mean the type of stations that still had signs about self-service, had rust everywhere, and had deep grooves the size of some ponds in their parking lots from years of trucker visits. There was always a scent of alcohol, cigarettes, lubricant, and shame in these places that seemed to punctuate just how out of place they were in comparison to even our small town much less larger cities. By the way, if this sounds like a very simple trip, that is because it was. It should have been a very uneventful drive, but then again, we had Zach with us.

Jordan and I were talking about a television show from a few nights before in the back of the F-150 when we heard a loud thump. Instinctively, we each looked up to see where we were, and noted that we seemed to be about halfway to the old bait and tackle shop. What we did not see at first was the source of the thump. We did, however, hear Lindsey start screaming and Lucky start laughing. I never liked the sound of screaming, but it sure caught my attention. After a couple seconds, Lindsey also started laughing, and we looked at each other wondering what was happening. As we turned back toward the front of the truck for another look, we finally saw Zach on the hood of the F-150 laughing like a lunatic.

Apparently, fueled by a very good joint, a couple of beers, and a dare from Abs, Zach decided to come visit us back in the F-150. While the two trucks sped along the highway, Zach climbed out of the passenger side of the S-10 while Brian signaled for Lucky to pull up closer to the S-10. Zach had then taken a running start in the bed of the S-10 and jumped onto the hood of the F-150. Apparently, this is where Lindsey screamed and Lucky, having seen Zach do this before we later learned, started laughing. Lindsey later said it was the coolest thing she ever saw, but Jordan and I just found it kind of odd and more than a little stupid. As we sat there staring at Zach, he climbed over the cab of the F-150, sat down between us, and said, "Hey, you fellas got a light?"

Zach proceeded to sit in the truck bed with us long enough to have a cigarette before climbing back over the cab, onto the hood, and then sitting up on the hood for a good couple miles of driving. After he grew bored, he planted his legs on the hood and leaped into the bed of the S-10, his momentum carrying him forward until he slammed into the back of the cab and we heard another loud thump. After a few moments where I wondered if he was conscious, Zach got up on his knees and with a wink and a wave in the direction of the trailing F-150 began climbing back into the S-10. I remember being amazed at the beating Zach's body could take in this and other moments of insanity. It was like he somehow developed much thicker skin than us lesser humans. According to Abs, the only thing he said when he entered the cab was, "Can I get another beer?"

The rest of the drive that day was uneventful. We arrived at the lake, got out of the trucks, laughed at Zach's crazy antics, and set up at a picnic site near the water. Throughout the rest of the day, we swam, laughed, drank beer, and ate the food we brought with us. At one point, I asked Zach about what looked like bruises all over his back and stomach, but he said, "Well, you know how it goes, you do crazy shit and it just leaves some marks, nothing to worry about," before walking over to the water by himself for a little while. Everyone other than Lindsey and I also smoked a lot of cigarettes and pot that afternoon. At one point, Lindsey asked me if I had ever smoked either, and I told her I had not. At that, she said she just didn't understand the appeal, and I couldn't disagree. All in all, it was a pretty unremarkable day at the lake to kick off the summer before high school for all of us except Abs. For Abs, it was the day she had sex for the first time.

CHAPTER 12

We left the lake around ten that night. As we were getting ready to go, Abs said she wanted to ride in the back of the F-150 with Jordan and I. We had not seen Abs in a couple of hours, and were curious what she had been up to. Plus, it was Abs – our regular partner in all kinds of crimes – so we were thrilled. Zach, on the other hand, did not seem too happy, but we figured that had nothing to do with us.

After some discussion between Zach, Lucky and Abs, she came over to the F-150 and hopped in the bed of the truck with us. It was starting to get chilly so the three of us snuggled up together – Abs in the middle unfortunately – in a blanket for the ride home. Abs kept giggling as the truck pulled onto the road, and finally, Jordan asked, "So where the hell were you?"

Without missing a beat, she said, "I was getting laid motherfucker," and burst out laughing while placing her head on Jordan's chest.

"What," we both said at the same time. We each stared at her, but she just laughed for a few minutes before trying to speak and then starting to giggle again.

Still giggling, Abs said, "I had sex, I did it, and I loved it!"

Earlier that day, we were all sitting around the picnic area talking about a whole lot of nothing when Lindsey grabbed Abs and took off down the beach. Lindsey had a habit of disappearing for a while so we thought nothing of it, and in a half hour or so she came back to where we were all swimming. She didn't say anything about where she went, and none of us bothered to ask. She was simply gone, and then she was back – not unusual for her or for us. Abs, however, did not return until it was time to leave the lake even though – to my knowledge – none of us really noticed at the time.

Apparently, Lindsey spotted a beach umbrella she recognized from the times her and her sister came to the lake over the years. This beach umbrella, it so happens, belonged to her sister's friend Veronica, and Lindsey wanted to go over and say hey to the group. When her and

Abs got to the spot where the other group was hanging out, they found Veronica and a whole lot of other older kids from our town catching some sun, having some beers, and chatting about their summer plans. Some of them were planning to stay in town all summer, some were moving to bigger cities for jobs, and others were just having fun at the lake. Abs and Lindsey dove right into the conversation, and spent some time hanging out with the group and catching Veronica up on all that Lindsey's sister had been up to since she dropped out of school the year before.

While Lindsey and Veronica were catching up, Mark arrived, and Abs struck up a conversation with him. They spent the day hanging out with the others, swimming in the lake, and finally kissing on the beach until Abs asked if there was somewhere more private they could go. As luck would have it, Mark had not only driven himself to the lake, but he had taken his mom's van because she needed his truck that day. He asked Abs if she wanted to go hang out in the van, and, "I swear I almost jumped out of my skin, like oh my god yes is what I wanted to say, but I played it cool."

"So, what happened next," I asked handing Jordan a soda.

"Well, we get into the van, and its one of those old style vans with lots of room – not that minivan type thing, but a big one. So, we're in the van making out, and he is such a good kisser and so cute and he says, I mean without me saying anything, he says, 'you know, we don't have to do anything but kiss, but we can if you want to.' I was blown away so I just told him the truth, you know, I said that I was a virgin, you know, but I wanted to have sex with him and you know, I had condoms and stuff so you know."

She stops for a second to light a smoke. It's a little tricky with all the wind beating against the truck as we fly down the road. We listen to the trees and the wind passing by in the nighttime. She says, "So he lays down the back seat of the van, and he leans me down on the seat, which is now kind of like a bed. And, you know, the radio picks that moment to play some Boyz II Men, and he starts kissing me softly on my neck, and I take off my top. I don't know why I did it, but it felt like the right time, and he just smiled and he started kissing me on my chest, very softly, then a little harder and a little harder. It felt so good, and I was just relaxing and enjoying his kisses thinking about that pretty body I told you about."

"Pretty body," Jordan asks.

"Yeah, he has a pretty body when he's naked, which Abs learned years ago. Keep up man."

Jordan just nods, and Abs giggles a little more and so do I.

She takes a puff off her cigarette, and continues, "So I'm breathing kind of hard, you know, like when Simon and I are rubbing against each other on the couch making out, you know? So I'm feeling good, and he starts to put his hand into my bikini bottom, but he stops and says, 'are you sure you want to do this' and I just kind of melted and I was like 'oh yes' like one of the girls in the movies or something. And so he just starts, and you know, oh my god that feels good, like so good! So, he's rubbing me, and I'm just like yes, and it kind of tickles but not really like being tickled, anyway, its fun and he's smiling and kissing me, and I just, oh my god."

She stops for a minute and just smiles up at the sky. She takes another puff off her cigarette, and says, "And then he starts to pull my bottoms off, and he starts, you know like you did with Lena, and it was really nice, I felt like warm. And he's doing this for a while and it feels good and then I just grab his hair, and at first, I'm like embarrassed because I didn't mean to do that so I start to say sorry and I say it like three times, but he's like 'it's cool, I like that' and then I just pull the shit out of his hair. And then, after a little while, he pulls his shorts off and grabs a condom out of his wallet and puts it on and I'm like, yeah!"

Jordan and I both start laughing, and she does too. "So then he asks me again if I'm sure, and I'm just like wow did I pick the right guy for this, you know? And I tell him yes, and he starts to, you know, it hurts a little bit and I wince. And when I wince, he pulls back for a minute and asks if I'm okay, and I just kiss him, and its nicer the second time, and he just keeps doing that for a few minutes you know, and it feels good, like really good. And then, after a few minutes, he starts shaking and he looks so cute, his eyes are all glazed over, you know. And he moans, I mean I made Mark moan, I'm that good, and he lays there with his head on my chest for a little while and I'm like oh my god, I did it, I really did it."

She takes another puff off her cigarette, and tosses it out of the cab. "Then, I reach for my cigarettes, you know, but he stops me. He takes out two of my cigarettes and lights them, and gives one to me – it was so cute, like something in a movie you know. Like, he just lights my cigarette all smooth, you know, it was cool. And we just lay there together and smoke and talk for a while, you know, not really saying nothing, but just, you know, hanging out or something I don't know. And then, after a while, he wants to go hang out with his friends, and I'm like, can I just stay here, and he's like yeah, stay as long as you want. So, he leaves and I just lay there and smoke and relax for a little while."

"So," Jordan asks, "How do you feel?"

She grins and hugs Jordan, "I feel great. I mean, I'm a little sore, you know, but I feel really good. That's why I had to ride home with y'all so I could enjoy this night, you know, I did it and I had fun and now I really want to do it with Simon when he gets back, you know, because that will be even more special you know."

"That sounds great Abs," I say, "What was up with Zach when we were getting ready to leave?"

"Oh, he's being stupid. We were kissing a little bit in the truck on the way out here, you know, it was kind of hot when he jumped between the trucks and so we were kissing a little bit, and I think he thought it was more than that or wanted more than that. It's no big deal."

"You kissed Zach? Really?"

"Shut up, don't ruin my moment – I'm a grown ass woman now."

Laughing, Jordan says, "I didn't know Mark's body had that kind of power," and we all laugh and snuggle under the blanket for a few minutes.

As the laughter starts to die down, I add, "Well it is pretty from what I've heard," and a fresh round of laughter ensues as we travel under the stars on our way back to the small town we call home for the next few years.

CHAPTER 13

The day after our trip to the lake I meet Jessica and Becca at the diner near our church. We get milkshakes – Oreo for me, chocolate for Jessica, and strawberry for Becca – and walk through the neighborhood behind the diner. Jessica and Becca are wearing the standard issue tank top with bikini top underneath and shorts combo so common in warmer states during the summer, and I am wearing one of Jordan's shirts and a pair of shorts. For some reason, I often end up noticing that I'm wearing Jordan's shirts when I hang out with Jessica these days. Part of me wonders about this pattern, but another part of me doesn't want to think about it.

"Where did you get that shirt," Becca asks me while tracing the Arabic lettering on the front of it. I don't know what it means. Neither does Jordan. His mom got it from one of the vendors out at the flea market over in Georgia. It looks beautiful, but for us, the words have no meaning at all.

"I don't remember," I lie.

"It's really cool, the lettering kind of jumps out at you. Do you know what it says?"

"No," the truth this time, "I have no clue."

"Oh, well, I like it."

Jessica is watching us and smiling. She takes a sip of her milkshake. She has often said it would be great if Becca and I could become like best friends, but unfortunately we often annoy the hell out of each other. Becca is making an effort, so I do the same.

"So, I heard you are going to a music camp later this summer. That sounds kind of cool."

"Yeah, it's a lot of fun. We all learn to play instruments and kind of jam out. It's like, really special, like, just hanging out with other girls rocking out to the music."

Jessica is smiling again. Okay, this is not so hard. "Well, what instrument are you going to play?"

"I think I'd like a drum set," Becca says, "I got a lot of aggression to let out, you know, I could be like a drummer and just bash the heck out of stuff. But I don't know, my parents want me to learn a more classical kind of instrument so I might do that instead."

"I don't know, I think the drums would be good for you."

Becca smiles. Jessica is smiling. This seems to be going well. I guess it is kind of odd that I have been dating Jessica for a long time now, and yet I barely know any of her friends beyond our little meetings at lunchtime during the school year. Last summer, I saw Jessica plenty, but had much less contact with the others. This summer, however, one of Jessica's friends has accompanied us each time we spent time together. I don't really care about Jessica's friends one way or another, but I guess I should at least try to be social sometimes if that is what she wants and her friends are willing.

In most cases, we basically do the same things. We meet up at church or at Jessica's house and then go walking around. We grab milkshakes or ice cream, and talk about whatever comes up along the way. It seems a bit odd that Jessica and I are never alone anymore, but I was enjoying her friends for the most part so it seemed like no big deal until we got to the park that day and Jessica went off to find a bathroom.

After she was gone, Becca turned to me, and asked, "Do you love her?"

"Huh, I mean, yeah, maybe, I think I do, I might, I don't know, why?"

"You better because she's thinking about," and in a whisper Becca says, "sex," and then she looks around for some reason, "And that is a serious thing so you better love her."

At this point, Jessica returns and Becca begins acting normal again as if our little conversation never happened. They decide to go to the area with the swings, and as they run off in that direction, I follow slowly. Suddenly, the constant chaperones make a lot of sense to me. Right before school ended, Jessica and I were making out on her couch like we have been for months now, and things got a little more heated than usual. At one point, her shirt ended up on the floor. We were both into the moment, and did not really talk about it at all. It just kind of happened, and then we heard her parents pulling into the garage, parted our bodies, and began acting like we were just watching a movie the whole time.

We have not been alone with each other since that day.

As I reached the swings, Becca's words rang in my head – do you love her. I really didn't know. I liked her a lot, like a whole lot, but do I love her? I knew I loved Jordan, but did I love Jessica? It wasn't the same kind of thing, and Jordan and I had a lot more time invested so it probably wasn't a fair comparison, but all I could think was that I did not feel as strongly for Jessica as I did for Jordan or even for Lena. Did that mean I didn't love Jessica? Or did that mean that I just loved Jordan a little more? I wondered what Lena was up to in Atlanta these days, and thought about giving her a call sometime. I didn't know if I loved Jessica, but suddenly it seemed like a very important question and I could not stop thinking about it.

I was trying to figure out an answer and watching the two of them swing when my heart fell out of my chest. On the other side of the playground, there was Jordan and he was walking this way. As if they were intentionally trying to make this more difficult, Becca and Jessica picked that moment to finish swinging, and Jessica came over and gave me a big kiss at the exact moment Jordan appeared to notice me in his path. I saw the hurt wash over his face. I felt sadness swallow me whole. He could have walked away, but he did not. Instead, he smiled a fake smile I had seen him use on his mother plenty of times, and said, "What's up mate?"

Why did he have to pick this moment to try to look strong? What was I supposed to do? Jessica was no help. She asked, "Do you know him," at about the same time Becca said, "Ooh, he's cute, does he have a girlfriend?" Yes he does, I thought, me.

Between a rock and a hard place, I said, "Hey Jordan, how you doing mate," as he got closer to where we were standing. I had always wondered what it would be like to see Jordan and Jessica at the same time, but this was not what I imagined.

"Not bad, not bad."

Turning to Jessica, I fought out the words, "This is my," I don't want to say this, shit, "friend" oh that hurt, "Jordan."

She said hello to Jordan, and he said hello to her.

Turning back to Jordan, I said, "And Jordan, this is my girlfriend," ouch, that hurt too, why did that hurt, "Jessica and her friend Becca."

With everyone acquainted, a bit of polite small talk ensued until Jordan excused himself and headed toward our spot near the woods. To anyone else, it probably appeared to be a perfectly natural interaction between a few teenagers, but I could see the pain he was hiding and fighting from the moment he decided to keep walking in our direction that day. The rest of our day continued like any other, but the whole time all I wanted to do was find Jordan and make sure he was okay.

CHAPTER 14

There is a little set of stairs that seem to go nowhere out behind one of the soccer fields at the park. In the middle of that summer, I was sitting on these steps looking down at the jogging track that circles the park and provides a kind of buffer between the park proper and the actual woods and neighborhoods beyond its borders. I was thinking about the exchange I had with Becca, and the moment Jordan, Jessica, and I stood in the same place for the first time.

I couldn't shake Becca's question or the painful feeling I got when I told Jordan Jessica was my girlfriend. Why was that painful? Did I love Jessica? Why was everything so complicated and how did it get this way? I had no clue what I was going to do, but I could not stop thinking about it no matter how hard I tried. Rather, all these questions played on a loop in my head until I heard a familiar voice.

"There's my silly boy," I heard Lena say before turning around to see her. I jumped to my feet and ran to her.

As we embraced, I asked, "What are you doing here?"

"I'm visiting silly – I'm quite the traveler these days," she said with a pout. "You looked like you were all deep in thought again over there, what's going on?"

"I'm confused again."

"About Jordan?"

"Yep, and about Jessica."

"Sounds about right, still having trouble figuring out which one you really want?"

Bracing myself for yet another session of advice about how I should just be with girls, I nodded, "I just don't know. I think I might love Jessica, but I know I love Jordan, and I know being with Jessica hurts Jordan and it hurts me to hurt Jordan, I don't know."

"I think you'll end up with Jordan, I mean, he's your first love and that is special."

Dumbfounded, all I could say was, "What?" This was the same girl who was so sure I couldn't like boys and girls, who was so sure that liking boys was a phase, who was so sure that Jordan was no big deal and something I would laugh about when I was older. What the hell did she just say? This was the same person who emphatically told me I needed a girl, and who even sought to demonstrate this in her bedroom many times. What the hell did she just say? Was this some kind of sick joke? What was happening?

Laughing, she says, "I don't know, I met this guy, Greg, in Atlanta, and it's kind of changed my opinions a bit. I mean, he has never once wavered in his feelings for other boys, and when he describes his feelings it sounds just like me talking about boys. I'm not kidding, he talks about boys and he sounds just like me, like exactly the same feelings and stuff since he was little. It seemed so strange to me at first, but then, I don't know, I started thinking maybe I was wrong, maybe people fall in love with different kinds of people or something. Maybe, it's just different kinds of the same thing or something. And then, I met his boyfriend and they are just like the perfect couple. I mean, perfect. I wish I could find guys who would treat me the way they treat each other, look at me like that, just perfect. His boyfriend likes boys and girls, you know like you, and I don't know, it seems to work. So, maybe Jordan is your Greg is all I'm saying."

My first thought was that maybe I needed to move to Atlanta. My next thought was a sense of relief I did not expect. For some reason, Lena saying what Jordan and I had might be real flooded me with a sense of confidence and surety that I did not expect. I didn't know what to say so I just stared off into the woods.

"Look, I'm just saying maybe the people in this town are wrong, you know, maybe I was wrong before, maybe what you're feeling is just natural." She lit a cigarette and put her arm around me, "If it is, maybe that's why you can't shake Jordan no matter who else you meet, you know, maybe he's not just a boy, maybe he's, you know, your first real love. Maybe the two of you are meant to be, and it seems strange just because no one taught us about it as kids."

I couldn't speak. It was like she left here and came back a completely different person. I just stared at her feeling things I couldn't really describe. I just loved her more than words in that moment, like even more than usual, and she was my childhood hero again.

I wanted to tell her how good it felt. I wanted to hug her. I wanted to say something, anything, but I just stared at her.

"Okay, that's enough of this mushy stuff," she said tossing her cigarette, "Some friends are hanging out down on the river so let's go have some fun."

I still didn't know what to say, but suddenly fun sounded like a really good idea. I put my arm in hers, and we semi-walked, semi-skipped toward the river just like we were kids again.

CHAPTER 15

The first day of high school arrived, and as was our tradition, Abs and I celebrated its ending by getting off the bus at the edge of our neighborhood and walking up to the magazine shop. Going to the magazine shop was different when Abs was with me because I wasn't ready for her to know what I did there when I was alone.

Instead of going to the back corner, I would go with Abs as she looked at this or that arts and music magazine, tried to determine which paperback novel she wanted to read before ultimately picking whichever Stephen King novel she had not read yet that would ultimately go straight to Jordan after she finished it because they were in love with the guy, and looked through the cassettes dissecting the merits of each one based on what the magazines, radio, and cover art could tell us about songs we had not yet heard. Sometimes, as we looked at other stuff, I would think about or even stare at the back corner, but if Abs ever noticed she didn't say anything and I didn't say anything. It was like I was a separate me when a witness was present, even if that witness was my best friend.

The fun part of these trips was that Abs was a great walking companion. She might find a stick to throw at something, yell random things at passing cars, or otherwise do something unexpected at any moment. I looked forward to seeing what types of mini-adventures would occur on the way, thought about the back corner of the store, and we walked down the sidewalk. She started singing a Madonna song and shaking her hips. Within a few seconds, we were both singing, "Open your heart to me" and dancing on the sidewalk.

After a few minutes, we both started laughing and had to stop for a minute. Standing on the sidewalk, Abs lit a cigarette, offered me one I didn't want, and just blurted out, "I had sex with Zach."

"What" I exclaimed and thought for a second I might need a cigarette for this one.

"We were at that barbecue last week, you know over at the Thompson's house, and he was being really stupid." The Thompson family had a little get together that pretty much everyone in the neighborhood went to each year to end the summer. They had this huge back yard situated right on the edge of the woods, and they basically let the whole neighborhood turn that yard into a dance floor, picnic area, and make out patch for one day each year. There were too many paper plates, hot dogs, soda cans, and cheesy pop songs playing from the stereo to count. There were kids everywhere, every age, and from every part of the neighborhood. The mass of people created a loud, chaotic goodbye to the freedom summer represented for folks of a certain age, and the Thompson's seemed to enjoy watching the insanity and having a captive audience for a handful of end of the summer speeches they always delivered.

"As usual."

"Yeah, but it was cute. He was showing the kids how to launch pinecones at their neighbors from the tree house, and it was just funny, you know."

I tried to imagine how teaching kids to weaponize pinecones could be sexually arousing, but I drew a blank. Maybe it was like the collecting panties thing, something I just couldn't understand the way others did. I was starting to realize that almost anything could be attractive to the right person, and while I found this comforting in some ways, it was also often confusing.

"Anyhow, after the barbecue, he walked me home, and my parents were still down in Charleston searching for the perfect Palmetto Rose." Her parents had a yearly tradition and a kind of obsession with Palmetto Roses, and they would spend hours – we counted one year when we made the mistake of leaving the beach early with them to see what they did – looking through the options to pick out the perfect ones – by some definition I never understood – to bring home for the front window of their house. They would also bring a few for my parents and some of the other neighbors. For a few weeks each fall, it would seem like Palmetto Roses were everywhere in the neighborhood. "So, he leaned in to try to get a kiss, you know how Zach is, and I just thought what the hell, you know, high school starts next week and Simon is still out of town and I wanted more than another boring night alone, so when he leaned in I kissed him, and asked if he needed to be home anytime soon."

"Look at you being all forward and confident."

"I know right, I'm awesome! I told you, I'm a grown ass woman now," and we laughed, grabbed each other's hands, and started walking again.

As we walked, I asked, "So, how was it?"

"Definitely not as good as Mark, but it was fun and he was actually a real gentleman, you know, he was kind and had condoms and held me afterwards. It was kind of sweet."

"Abs, body so awesome it can conquer the most annoying Zach," I said and started laughing. I said, "Glad you had fun."

"What about you, any juicy new details?"

"Nope, I'm just plain old boring."

"You and Lena didn't do anything while she was in town?"

"Not anything like that, we talked and drank some wine she brought from Atlanta and just hung out like back in the old days." At this point, we started to pass the gas station located right before the shopping center. "I think we both just kind of wanted to be together again without anything to worry about." As I spoke these words, we turned left and began to walk through the parking lot of the gas station. "We just kind of..." and then I stopped talking and just stared at the edge of the parking lot.

Roger was putting air in his tires. He looked like he had not shaved in a while and his clothes seemed very dirty, but otherwise he was just like I remembered him from the time Jordan introduced us at the park or times I'd seen him at the magazine shop discussing collectibles. He had bags under his eyes and the jovial grin he wore the other times I'd seen him did not seem to exist anymore. He just looked like a sad, or maybe angry, old man. His body seemed to just kind of be in his way, like he was tired of carrying it. I couldn't explain it, but he looked like he was the one who died even though he was still alive, I don't know, it was a feeling.

"Kind of?"

Catching my breath, I said, "Oh, uh, just kind of had fun like when we were younger."

Following my gaze, Abs said, "Oh, that poor man. Did you hear what happened? He was married to this other guy for like 30 years or something, I mean like forever, and the other guy got killed by some assholes in a parking lot." Of course, I heard all about it, and I still had trouble thinking about it, but I just stayed quiet. I didn't know how to talk about this without giving away how I really felt. It was like talking about this, seeing Roger here, scared me almost as much as what happened. Luckily, Abs was only taking a breath and did not actually need any commentary on my part.

"It's just terrible, how do you keep going after something like that? And what's worst, my mom and the other people at the church think it's his fault because he's gay – I couldn't believe my mom would say such a thing. How would she feel if it was my dad? What if I was gay, you know, what the hell?" I remembered Linda's description relayed to me by Jordan, and I marveled at the difference in the ways people could see things. Abs had been taught the same stuff we all had, and did not feel like we did to the best of my knowledge, but somehow she reacted differently than the other people who were not like us. I wondered how she did that.

She kicked the dust in the parking lot, and continued, "I don't know what I would do if I shared my whole life with someone and they were just taken from me, it's crazy sad, you know, I just want to hug him and make it all better, you know, I wish there was something we could say to him, you know, something we could do."

Tears rolling down my face, I said, "I'm in love with Jordan."

Turning slowly, everything seemed to be moving so slow in that moment, Abs looked at my face, saw my tears, opened her eyes wide in surprise, and then gave me one of the greatest presents of my life. She reached around me, pulled me close to her, and said, "I love you, you hear me, and I'll kill anyone who ever tries to hurt you," and we just stood there, so close that I could distinguish between the smell of smoke and the smell of hairspray as my nose grazed the side of her head, for what seemed like the longest moment of peace I'd ever known.

CHAPTER 16

Jordan was sitting in the grass as I approached our spot at the end of the first week of high school. He didn't see or hear me from what I could tell. He was just staring off in the direction of the ball fields, rocking back and forth, and somehow shining in the moonlight. I never could figure out how that happened, but he always seemed to be lit up with different lights than the rest of us, like he existed in another space alongside the rest of the world where colors were brighter and more, I don't know, alive or fresh or something. It was amazing. For a moment, I just stopped and stared at him as I often did in such moments. It was almost like I was trying to soak it in, create a personal photograph in my own memory, and explore the nuances in it for a few seconds. He looked so peaceful that I just wanted to capture the moment and hold onto it forever.

When I started moving again, he heard me and turned around with a smile. He waved, slightly extending his hand, and wiped a bit of sweat from his lips. I sat down beside him, and he put his hand in my lap where I grasped it with my own fingers, softly pecked me on the cheek, and said, "So how was your first week?"

We had not seen each other or spoken that week. I guess we were both busy getting back into the swing of school or getting used to all the changes taking place or maybe we just needed time away sometimes even from each other. I missed him when we didn't talk, but it also made it even more fun when the silence ended. I touched his cheek, and said, "I told Abs I'm in love with you."

"You did?" I couldn't make out his face in the dark. I couldn't tell how he felt about the news. I hoped he would not be mad. Jordan was much more sensitive to the danger we were dancing with than I was at the time, and he rarely shared anything private with anyone. In many ways, I was probably the only one who really knew much about him at that point.

"Yeah, I didn't plan it, it just kind of happened. We saw Roger and she started talking about how sad what happened was and how she wished she could make it all better, and I just kind of blurted it out without thinking. I didn't tell her anything about you. I just told her that I was in love with you."

With a softness in his voice that I knew meant he realized I was nervous, he said, "So how did she react?"

"She just kind of hugged me, like really hugged me tight, and said she loved me and wouldn't let anyone hurt me. It was really nice. I was really overwhelmed by the sight of Roger, and so it was really good to not feel alone for a minute."

"How was Roger doing?"

"We didn't talk to him, I was too upset. He looked like he was dying, or had just given up or something. He was a mess Jordan, he looked miserable, and I barely recognized the happy guy he used to be. It was scary to see how much he has changed. It was just terrible. He still looked like himself, the old guy obsessed with collectible jewelry, but, I don't know, it was like a part of him was missing or something."

Jordan just nods like he expected this, or maybe he already knew. Maybe he visited Roger. I thought about asking, but instead I said, "It was just bad, and I felt horrible and I think that's why I just blurted out how I felt when Abs started talking about wanting to make it better somehow, I don't know, it just happened."

"That's good. How do you feel about it?"

"I feel good, I think its good that I told her and I think I can trust her with it the same way I trust her with all the other stuff and she trusts me with her stuff." I could see him nodding, and I continued, "She also told me she had sex with Zach."

"I know."

"You know?"

"Yeah, Zach was bragging about nailing her all week in the locker room."

"The locker room?"

"Yeah, I'm on the basketball team now, and so I spent a lot of time in the locker room with the other guys this week."

"Wow, that's cool. How did that happen?"

"They needed another player for the team, and Zach recommended me to the coach. So, I'm going to be on the team, but I probably won't play. It's kind of nice though because people treat you kind of awesome when you're on the team. I don't know, I'm popular now instead of the butt of guy's jokes."

"That sounds great! How is the locker room?"

"Oh, its really nice – the guys are all mostly naked, but no one notices if you look at each other because everyone kind of has to look at each other in the small space. So, its like a great view, but also it feels very safe. It's weird, because you know how the guys make all those jokes about guys like me, and they do that in the locker room too, I mean a lot. But, I don't know, it feels different, not really scary at all, in there. Its like I'm in on the joke even though I'm the joke, I don't know, its interesting, kind of nice and not at the same time if that makes any sense. I was worried about it, I mean, I didn't know what it would be like to be around all the boys like that, but it is actually kind of nice and after the first day, it kind of just felt normal, like maybe I could belong there or something."

"You got a favorite teammate big boy?"

His voice taking on a harder tone that makes me feel a little bad, he says, "No. I don't need a Jessica."

"Are you still mad at me?" He doesn't respond, but he takes his hand away from my lap. "What am I supposed to do Jordan? You don't want us to be together, you don't want me to be with Jessica, do you want to pick someone else for me? What do you want?" He doesn't respond, I hate it when he gets quiet like this and he knows that – asshole. We have been having this same conversation on the phone, and he always has to get off the phone at this point, but not tonight, I want answers. "What do you want Jordan? You know I love you, you know you love me, so if you want it to just be us all you gotta do is say so. What do you want?"

He sighs, and gets up from the grass. Before he can start to walk away, which I know is what he was going to do, I grab him by the arm and stand up right in front of him. "What do you want Jordan? You know what I want, I told you last week on the phone. It's your turn big boy, what do you want?"

He tries to turn away from me, but I'm tired of this back and forth so I grab him and make him look at me face to face. He is shaking, and I hate that I know I'm making things hard for him, but I also can't keep having this argument. "What do you want?"

He pulls away from my grip, and says, tears choking his voice, "You know what I want? I want to stop being afraid. I want to stop thinking about Daniel. I want to just hold your hand on the way to school like all the boys and girls get to do. I want to stop feeling so damn alone all the damn time. I want to kiss and cuddle and go to dances with you. Okay, that's what I want. I want to be able to be honest with everybody without being afraid of how they'll react. I want to do all the things everybody else gets to do damn it! That's what I want, there, are you happy now? Are you?"

I just stand there quietly fighting the urge to apologize, the desire to protect him like I usually do. I just stand there.

"You know what I don't want? I don't want you to have to choose between hiding with me and getting to do all that other stuff. I don't want to make you hide too. I don't want you to have to put up with all my shit! I don't want someone to hurt you because they find out I love you. I don't want to have to choose between lies and danger every damn day, that's what I don't want! I don't want to wonder if the churches are right about us, okay, I don't want to wonder if hell is real! Sometimes I don't want to feel this way at all anymore, sometimes I want to be able to like both like you do or maybe just like girls, that has to be easier than this shit! I don't want to take that away from you, but I don't want anyone else to touch you either. I don't want to find out later that I'm not enough because you need a girl too. I don't want to be so confused and angry and worried, okay, I don't want that at all! I don't want to feel so damn angry all the time, I don't want it to hurt so much, and I don't want a favorite teammate unless its you don't you get that you asshole!"

Out of nowhere, Jordan, the least violent person I have ever known, hauls off and starts punching the tree with all his might. I rush to him and put my arms around him from behind, and block the punches, but his hands are already starting to bleed. He punches against my hands a few more times, and then collapses to the ground. His whole body is shaking, he doesn't notice he has obviously hurt his hands, he just shakes and shakes, and I wish I could take it all away and make it all better, but I know I can't. So, I just stay there, hold him, and wait. I don't know what else to do. I continue to hold him as he sobs and says, "I'm sorry, I'm so sorry, I'm so sorry, make it go away, please make it go away, please," until he finally runs out of breath and just sits there motionless in my arms, in the grass, in the cool night air, in our spot.

CHAPTER 17

At Sunday school that weekend, I walk in and automatically go to one of the smaller rooms where we have our lessons. I don't feel like seeing anyone or dealing with the social rituals that make up the beginning of the Sunday school time period. Jessica sees me when I enter the larger, outer room, and watches me go into the smaller lesson room without saying anything. In fact, no one says anything. They all seem to be chatting anxiously about something around the table with the food. I'm grateful for this lucky break.

After about a half an hour of sitting motionless and silent in the grass the other night, Jordan asked me if I could handle being with only one person. I told him that if that person were him there would be nothing to handle because it was what I wanted most in the world. He started to apologize for becoming so upset, but I told him that it was actually nice to finally be sure that this stuff was as hard for him as it was for me. He started crying again, and said he didn't want me to have to choose, to be something I wasn't, and he kept trying to be strong and keep it all to himself. I told him choosing him was who I was, and that he should have told me how he felt sooner instead of trying to be a macho jerk.

We sat there talking for a long time. We talked about many different things, and we shared a lot of what we were feeling both when we were and were not around each other. We talked about Jessica and the storeroom and Lena and the boy from his camp. We talked about Roger and Daniel, and how scared we were that we could end up like that. We talked about his mom always telling him about cute girls she saw at work, and we talked about Linda. We talked about Abs and Lena and how much their support helped me. We talked about Jessica and how I felt and how Jordan felt about her. We talked about how lonely it was to be like us in this small town. We talked about a lot of things that night, but only one thing really mattered. At some point, in the middle of other topics, Jordan finally asked me to be with only him and I said yes.

With all this fresh in my mind, I spent the whole next day and the ride to Sunday school this morning trying to figure out what to say to Jessica. It was hard to figure out because on the one hand I was happier than I had ever been about the upcoming breakup, but on the other hand, I really cared about Jessica – if not nearly as much as I did about Jordan – and I did not want to hurt her. I also had no clue what I should say if she asked me why I wanted to break up. In small town South Carolina, "I'm in love with a wonderful man," was not exactly a safe response to that question. I didn't know what to say, but I knew I wanted to get it over with.

While I was trying to figure it out, Becca and Jessica came into the little room, and Becca asked, "Did you hear?"

"Hear what," I asked genuinely curious.

"Well, "what's-his-name," he was in our study group before he moved to the other one a while back." I wanted to say, you mean right after I had sex with him in the storeroom. "His parents came home early from vacation, and found him in bed with a guy." After the word guy, which Becca said with a distinct sound of distaste in her mouth, she began to laugh and so did Jessica. Maybe ending this relationship would be easier than I thought because at that moment I kind of wanted to hurt both of them. They were talking about a nightmare for people like us, even assholes like what's his name, and they thought it was funny. Once she finished laughing at the thought of what's his name with a guy, Becca continued, "It was that boy Tim that used to go to our school before he got kicked out for fighting. Remember him? He was cute, long black hair, but was always fighting and angry." I never really noticed Tim, but being angry all the time made a lot of sense to me especially if liking guys was something he always felt. "What's his name's parents showed up, and they walked in on the two of them, like, doing it, like all the way. Well, they about lost their minds, and they chased the guy out of the house and brought what's his name to the church right away."

I remember being surprised that despite how he treated me after the storeroom, I felt really bad for what's his name in that moment. He was a jerk as far as I was concerned, but the things we were feeling in that storeroom were terrifying in this little town, and getting caught was a nightmare I didn't want to consider at any point. I didn't know what that would be like, but I knew it was not going to be good and I wondered if there was any way to help him or get him out of here, but I knew there was nothing I could really do. Our church was not what one would call liberal under the best of circumstances, and homosexuality in our church was never the best of circumstances. "What did they do?"

"Well, they agreed that he was sick, like, messed up, and so they sent him to this camp for kids who are confused about sex." Sick. There was that word I had heard so many times in my life already by that point. They thought we were sick when we fell in love with people they did not approve of is the way Jordan put it. Sick, what an evil word? "It's okay though, they said that the camp can cure him, and he'll be back to church good as new." Cure him, like he is sick, yep, heard this song and dance before, and still hated it. I felt an overwhelming urge to tell them both that I was like what's his name just to see how they might react, but I didn't do it. I knew it would do no good.

Jessica said, "It's got to be so hard for his family. They didn't even know he was, you know, messed up like that, and now the whole church knows. That's why my mom was saying we all need to pray for them now because they really need our support."

I found myself just staring at the two of them, and it dawned on me that suddenly Jessica seemed much less beautiful than she had before today. What's his name was being attacked for liking a boy, and his parents were the ones who needed our support? Who the hell was this girl? Would she say the same about me, about Jordan? I wondered what she thought about Roger and Daniel? Did they even know about that? How did I not know her feelings on this subject? I certainly never imagined she would ever sound like Linda the night Daniel died. Before I could say anything, the other kids started pouring into the room. Not surprisingly, the teacher announced that we would be talking about Leviticus that day.

CHAPTER 18

As I did whenever anything major happened in my life, that night I
went over to Abs' house and knocked softly on her window. She peered
through the blinds, smiled at me, and waved toward the back yard. We
had been doing this for years. Abs had a lot of time to herself at home,
and so her house was ground zero for us whenever we didn't want or
have time to go out to the river. I would sneak out of my window two
blocks away, and walk to her house. I went to the window because the
one time we almost got caught meeting late at night was due to the
lighting at the front door her parents insisted on when they were out or
asleep. So, I met her at the window, and she would motion me to the
back yard. We would sit up and just enjoy the night and talk about all
the things kids had to talk about.

Once outside, she said, "Well don't I feel special – two
gentlemen callers in one night."

"Two?"

"Yes, your boyfriend was over here earlier."

Boyfriend? He told her. Jordan told someone about us? Really?
I was shocked. I was amazed. I was even more in love than usual with
him. I just stared at Abs.

Laughing, she said, "Yeah, that's how he thought you would
react. Apparently, our little Jordan is not good at talking about
feelings." Lighting a cigarette and offering me one that I turned down,
she added, "He said he wanted me to know that he was gay and that
he was in love with you too because he didn't want you to have to
hide your relationship from me anymore. He thinks you need me, and
I happen to agree. I think he needs me too or someone other than you
to share with, but our Jordan will never admit that."

"I don't know what to say."

"Considering how private Jordan is and how scared he seemed
to be, I think you should just say 'wow' and think about how much he
must care about you to be willing to walk all the way to my house just
to tell me his biggest secret so that I can be there for you. I gotta admit,
that's pretty impressive. What if I would have been like the people at

the church? I mean, that took guts, and he did it for you." She takes a puff off her smoke, "Maybe this is Jordan's first steps toward feeling okay about himself and what the two of you have." Maybe Abs was right, but then again, Abs wondered if Jordan was "like that" for years so for her this was confirmation more than anything else, and she was enjoying being right as much as she always did. She takes another puff, punches me in the arm hard, and says, "And that's for lying to me for years even though I understand why you did and I would have done the same, damn animals in this town, but still, it sucks that you felt you had to lie to me so I had to get that out. I always wondered about Jordan, but I'm still kind of surprised about you."

I couldn't resist, "Why Jordan and not me Abs?"

Laughing, she says, "This is going to sound terrible, but Jordan just kind of fits, you know. He is never with girls, he never says much but always looks put together, he reminds me of Matt on Melrose Place, okay? I mean, they obviously don't look the same, but you know, some of the same tendencies and stuff. I don't know, you know, I just wondered about him, and remember in fifth grade I was sure he had a crush on you."

"You also thought I had a crush on you in fifth grade."

"Shut up, I know, but Jordan just always seemed like he was keeping something back – the same way Zach does now, but I don't think it's the same – and the way he looked at you, I don't know."

"But you had no clue about me?"

"You know, you are the girliest person I have ever met, but that's probably a stereotype because Matt on Melrose Place is not all that girly. You know, I don't think I ever considered it really, you know, you've kind of always been mine, you know, not like that, but mine and I guess I never thought about it. Maybe I should have. Honestly, I always thought you and Lena would end up together when we all grew up. I imagined the two of you in some big city drinking wine on a balcony and making fun of this small town."

"Lena, really?"

"The two of you were always just so cute together, and always around each other. Of course, I could say the same thing about Jordan now that I think about it. You know, maybe this town got to me, I don't know, you know, I just never thought about it. I probably would have if I'd been more, you know, open, but shit, I never did. Does that make me horrible?"

"No, I think that just makes you a product of this place, like the rest of us. There are probably all kinds of things out in the world we don't even imagine yet."

"You're probably right, but I still don't like that I never even considered it with you and him even though I thought about it with you and her. It just seems wrong, and I should be better than that, you know? Speaking of things I never thought about, did you hear about what's his name?"

"Yeah, I did. The guy is a jerk, but I still feel bad for him."

"I didn't know you knew him that well. I remember seeing y'all hanging out at church, but I didn't know you were ever close."

Putting my finger in my mouth, and smiling, I say, "Yep we were close for a few minutes."

Abs almost falls off her porch because of how hard she starts laughing. "And I'm the conqueror of men," she finally says.

I laugh too, and then say, "So, I broke up with Jessica."

"How did it go?"

"It was actually pretty easy. It turns out she thinks people like what's his name are sick and in need of prayer. I caught up with her alone at church tonight, and told her I didn't think we should see each other anymore. She asked why, and I just kind of shrugged. She'll probably hate me now, but even if Jordan and I weren't together now I don't think I could look at her the same way knowing what she thinks about people like what's his name."

"You mean people like you and Jordan."

"Yep. People like us. I guess I just never imagined she would feel that way, I mean, I guess I thought she was better than that. Anyway, after I just shrugged, she kind of started tearing up and talking about our special bond and I was still angry from earlier in the day so I just said that we didn't have any kind of bond. I told her it was just a middle school thing, but middle school was over and I needed to move on, be with someone more grown up. It was mean, but I was just angry and I just wanted it to be over."

"Yeah, I get it. Hell, I would have probably said worse if I were you, but you always were too nice for your own good." This is Abs' main criticism of me. Abs believes everyone who is not nice should be destroyed, but I tend to try to avoid conflict. Abs says its because I have an overly optimistic view of people, but I don't think that's true. I just don't think most of the fighting matters in the end. Abs disagrees, and will fight everything in sight if it stands in her way or hurts someone. I'm too nice, and she's too much like the Terminator, but maybe that's the kind of friend we both need.

"Maybe, I don't know, I just didn't want to hurt her, but then after what she said I kind of did want to hurt her. I don't know."

"Well, breakups suck, but it could be worse," she says and lights another cigarette.

"You think?"

"Sure, you're not the one who had sex with Zach again," she says before taking a long puff on her cigarette and rolling her eyes.

"You didn't?"

"I don't know man, there is just something adorable about him, I don't know what it is but I kind of like, you know, just how sweet he is in bed compared to just how much of an asshole he is the rest of the time. There is also something, this is horrible, don't judge me, there is something about his body that is so much man, you know, he's always covered in cuts and bruises from whatever the hell he does when we're not together and his muscles are just so tight – thank you basketball – I don't know, it's just kind of hot. Who knows, maybe I'm the sick one."

"You said it," I say with a grin, and she promptly punches me in the arm. "What, I can't pretend to understand how anyone is attracted to that idiot, but I love you and at least we know that down beneath all the crap, Zach's a pretty good dude who worships you." Laughing, I say, "Who knows, maybe Zach is your one true love."

"Don't make me really hurt you," she says with a giggle. "Wouldn't that just be the craziest shit," she asks, and I can't disagree.

CHAPTER 19

The rest of the first semester of high school flew by like a spirited wind leaving nothing but memories behind in the dust. I spent most of my spare time with Jordan just hanging out and laughing and kissing a whole lot. Jordan and I would meet at our spot, and go walking in the woods like we always had, but somehow it felt different now, more serious, more real. Sometimes, Abs would come with us, and the three of us would talk about music and school and the fact that Abs kept occasionally having sex with Zach even though she was always sure it was the last time and it meant nothing.

Other times, Jordan and I just retreated into our own world. He would swipe wine bottles from his mom's collection after she had too much to drink so she wouldn't notice, and we would sip from the bottle out by the river like newlyweds in a romantic comedy. We would go down to our little path that we kept hidden in plain sight, and take naps by the stream. Jordan would sleep with his head on my chest, and I would play with his hair and watch his dark brown skin glisten in the sunshine. We wrote each other notes that we traded at my bus stop when he passed on his way to school in the mornings or on his way home in the afternoons.

The notes were never anything special. We stuck to our rule of being careful about evidence. They never had our names on them, but just talked about the latest gossip, our days, and songs. To anyone else, they probably looked like simple little notes kids pass all the time in school. We came up with a code where the talk about songs was actually how we felt about each other. We would find songs that expressed how we felt and share lyrics and thoughts on the lyrics. Nothing was ever explicit in these little notes, but we both knew what it meant, and we both looked forward to the next one.

At other times, I would go out to Jordan's school to watch him play basketball. Every time I did this, Abs came with me and said we were there because she wanted to watch Zach shake his little butt in those shorts. This way, she explained, nobody would think it was strange for me to be at the games. I was just her buddy who made sure she didn't have to sit alone while she watched Zach play. In reality, I never saw much of the games. I spent the whole time watching Jordan ride the bench. I kept hoping he would get to play, but only because I wanted to watch him run in the little shorts. Hell, even Zach looked sexy to me in those little shorts, dripping sweat, and running up and down the court.

Abs' parents worked night shifts at the fiberglass plant so she often had the place to herself in the early and late evenings. The same way I would knock on her window to chat for years, Jordan and I would come by separately on those evenings, and the three of us would hang out on the back porch or watch movies on the couch. Sometimes Zach was there, and we would have to play it as friends, but other times it would just be the three of us and we would get to cuddle – with each other and Abs – during the movies. When Simon was there, Abs would usually take him into her room after about an hour so they could have sex, talk, or do whatever they wanted alone, and Jordan and I would have the whole house to our selves.

Right after the semester ended, just before Christmas, Jordan's mom got a new job. It was a major step up for her. She now worked the desk at the fancy hotel in Augusta, and made pretty good money without having to deal with drunks looking for their last beer of the night. The best thing about this job, however, was that it meant she started work each night at 10 and did not get back home until around 9 the next morning. Almost immediately, Jordan and I had our own place to cuddle and watch movies because she would leave the house around 8 each night to get coffee at the diner before her shift. While we would still go over to Abs' house on some nights, other nights we met at our spot, walked over to Jordan's place, and cuddled up on the couch. From that couch, we watched January and February of our first year of high school disappear.

Jordan's mom was in especially good spirits because of the new job. After witnessing what happened to Daniel, she never felt safe again at the store, especially at night. One of her friends from years before had come back to town to work for the hotel – "That smarty pants became an accountant" she would say – and contacted her to catch up. Over drinks, she told him about her job, and he asked if she wanted a position at the hotel. That was how she ended up serving the rich people that visited the area to see the farms, the nuclear plant, the golf tournaments, and the horse races every year. She would stand or sit behind this massive oak counter wearing a fancy button down shirt – "It was like I was at church," she would say giggling over her wine – and get paid to flirt with rich older men and to compliment the outfits of rich older ladies. Apparently, this did not constitute flirting with the women according to her view of the world. As she told us one afternoon between glasses of wine, she felt, "Like things are finally working out for me." We celebrated with her even though we were much more thrilled with our newfound ability to cuddle as much as we wanted without fear.

Jordan's mom also seemed especially happy that he found himself a nice girl. Of course, she did not know that the girl's name – Emily – he told her was actually a pseudonym for me, but it was still nice to hear her talk about how wonderful Emily must be. My parents felt the same way about Jane – a name Jordan chose because he thought Jane Fonda was the coolest girl ever next to Abs, Lena, and me. Emily had been invented when Jordan's mom noticed him acting different around the house. He was listening to love songs, agonizing over what to wear to school, and smiling a lot. As is often the case, his mom assumed he met a girl, and asked him about her. On the spot, Jordan would later say it was out of desperation and fear, he invented a girl named Emily that went to school with him who he spent time with between classes. His mom was intrigued so he added to the story more and more until his mom came to believe he had a crush on a girl named Emily who was not allowed to really date until she was 16 – so mom could not meet her – but was crazy about her son. Jordan and I would giggle every time his mom brought up Emily, and we noticed she was much more welcoming to my constant presence in the house after Emily's creation was established as a background detail of her son's life. We had fun creating Emily, and spent a lot of time working out the details of her life, personality, and interest in Jordan, fashion, and basketball.

When March rolled around, we were cuddled up in what was becoming the usual manner the week before my fifteenth birthday. I had my head on Jordan's chest, and he was playing with my hair while we watched an old comedy. I was thinking about how soft his hands were and how nice the wine we swiped from his mom tasted when he said, "What are you doing on your birthday," before leaning down and kissing me softly on my head.

"I don't really have any plans for that day. As usual, my parents will probably want me to have dinner with them and eat some cake, but then I can do anything."

"I was thinking we should hang out here that night."

"But your mom doesn't work on Saturday nights."

"I know, but she will be in Atlanta all weekend with the other hotel staff. I thought it would be nice to make it a special night."

"I'd love to spend my birthday with you."

CHAPTER 20

On the night of my birthday, I dressed as nicely as I knew how, and walked to Jordan's house. Instead of meeting in our usual spot, he asked me just to come to the house. I didn't know it at the time, but Jordan had been planning this night for months.

He went to see Roger to learn about sex, lubrication, condoms, and other aspects of love making. He even called Lena for advice, and she put him in contact with Greg who, despite losing his perfect boyfriend to a case of boredom, was happy to share the vast amount of information he had on the subject. He practiced putting on condoms, putting lubricant on himself, and moving his body in certain ways that he learned from a stack of videos and magazines Roger let him have. He spent months collecting candles, and hiding them in his closet so he could light the room in a special way. He burned many failed attempts at macaroni and cheese to learn how to make it the way I liked it, and he had been hiding some of the wine he borrowed from his mom under his bed. I didn't know it, but Jordan was finally ready to open up to me in every possible way.

Jordan and I had been talking about sex since long before either of us had any of it in our lives. We also talked about having sex with each other many times, but Jordan was not sure if he ever wanted to do it again – with anyone – after his experience at camp. He had been so shaken up that he didn't even enjoy kissing for a little while after that first time. He would be the first to admit that his first time was with someone nice, kind, and sweet, but there was something about being so vulnerable, naked, exposed that bothered him. He all but swore off of sex even though in time he did start kissing and cuddling again. I wanted to be with Jordan that way for as long as I could remember having any feelings about that way, but I also expected that it would either never happen or only happen a long way in the future. I couldn't understand what he was feeling, but I decided it didn't matter if I could understand it, I could wait forever as long as we were together in the ways we could be.

I walked through the park listening to some generic rock music on my Walkman. I couldn't stop smiling thinking about a whole night with Jordan. I didn't care what we did, what we talked about, or what Jordan had planned. I had long made peace with the fact that we were, as Abs put it, "Taking things slow," and I just wanted to spend the night wrapped in his arms. I smiled at the flowers that seemed brighter, and laughed at the families playing in the park hoping they were having the time of their lives. I finally got to the edge of Jordan's block, and I felt like my heart was beating out of my chest. I just knew it would be a night I would never forget.

Instead of sex, what I was thinking about were feelings. Jordan was not very good at talking about how he felt, but he had been doing better since the night he beat up the tree. I was thinking that maybe tonight he would be romantic, tell me how he felt about me, talk about a future together, that kind of stuff. I was imagining a long time together spanning decades, and I was thinking maybe Jordan was having the same thoughts and would tell me about it. At the same time, a small part of me was also hoping for sex or at least maybe a conversation about sex. I was fine with how things were, but at the same time, I regularly had dreams about us being together like that, and I found myself thinking about those dreams and feelings the whole way to Jordan's house.

Jordan was inside the house lighting candles. He was checking and re-checking the bedroom, the food he made in the kitchen, the wine bottles and corkscrew, and everything in the house. He was wearing a pair of khaki pants that looked amazing on him, and a white button down shirt that complimented his dark skin tone and had just enough room between the buttons to hint at his chest. He was barefoot, as he always was inside the house, but he fixed his hair – something he never did – for the occasion. He looked like everything beautiful in the world when he opened the door.

Before I walked up to the door, I stood across the street for a little while smiling and thinking about how nice it was to look forward to my birthday. Normally, I saw my birthday as more like a hassle or a let down than anything else. My parents would get me a cake – the same one every year – and a couple presents that I didn't really want, and we would have dinner. That was it. There were never any parties, surprises, or anything like that as far as I can remember. It was just another day, but it happened to have the same cake I kind of liked but not all that much every year. This year was different. This year, it felt like my birthday was special.

I felt nervous. What if I wasn't dressed right? What if I messed up the evening somehow? What if I said or did the wrong thing? What if we had sex and I wasn't any good at it? What if I knocked on the door only to find out that Jordan forgot about tonight? What if his mom was home? A thousand what if questions kept running through my head, and finally, I just said who cares and walked to the door. I felt this way earlier in the day, and went to see Abs to make sure I looked okay, have a sip of the wine she was drinking, and hear her say everything would be wonderful. I sat there with Abs thinking please be right again, please, please please, oh knower of everything get this one right. At Jordan's house, nerves and fantasies colliding in a too small space within my head, I stood there shaking, and then I knocked on the door.

The door opened, and Jordan smiled at me in the way only he could at that time in my life. He looked perfect, and he sounded perfect when he said, "Happy birthday honey," and came through the door to wrap his arms around me, kiss me hard on the mouth, and smack me on my butt. I started giggling, overcome with joy, and let him lead me into the house. I felt like my skin was vibrating, and all I wanted to do was soak up the wonderful feelings pulsing through my whole body at that moment and somehow keep them forever.

When we got in the house, I saw candles everywhere. There were also two glasses of wine on the coffee table, and what looked like freshly made macaroni and cheese sitting beside two matching plates on the table in the cut out that was supposed to be a dining room. Looking nervous, Jordan asked, "Do you like it?"

Choking on tears, I said, "Yes, I love it so much."

Jordan's whole body relaxed, and he reached over and turned on the stereo. From the speakers, one of my favorite records began to play, and Jordan reached out for my hand. In moments, we were dancing in the living room, and somehow it felt like a ballroom or a movie set or some kind of paradise far away from our little town. Our bodies swayed together effortlessly like they had so many times in the woods where no one could see, and his hands on the small of my back felt like electricity come to life, captured in a moment, created just for us. I ran my hands through his hair, and he kissed me, softly at first, then harder as we moved in rhythm to the song. The world fell away, and for the entirety of side one of the record, it was just the two of us without fear, without worry, without anything to get in the way of our shared need to be close to each other.

When side one ended, Jordan stepped to the player, and turned the record over. As side two began, he pulled my face to his and we kissed in the glow of the candles. As the songs played, I slowly unbuttoned his shirt. Our bodies continued to move to the music, and I savored the sweet taste of his skin on my lips like I found the greatest ice cream ever created. Jordan knew this was one of my favorite things, and I knew he enjoyed it. Usually, it was as far as our make out sessions would go, and so it felt like a kind of climactic event every time. I felt my head begin to spin, as if I was intoxicated even though I wasn't, and then Jordan did something he had never done before.

Hesitantly, fingers trembling a little bit, he started unbuttoning my shirt, and with one hand he raised my head to where our eyes locked. Softly, he whispered, "I love you so much," before beginning to kiss my chest, and my neck. The second side of the record ended, but I barely noticed – I had been waiting so long for this moment. Jordan was touching me in ways I only dreamed he would. All I could register was the beautiful exhilaration of Jordan's lips. He turned me slowly so he could pull off my shirt.

The room was silent except for my breathing. The candles burned and so did I. The beauty of the moment seemed to swallow me whole, and I began moaning softly as he rubbed my shoulders with his hands. After a while, he turned me back around and we kissed like it was the first time. When our lips finally parted, he took me by the hand, and led me to his bedroom leaving his own shirt in the hallway between the living room and his bedroom door.

As we walked toward the bedroom, I was quite sure my heart would explode. I didn't think we would do anything more than we were already doing, but we never went in the bedroom when we were making out. We always separated the spheres of contact because Jordan was uncomfortable with what might happen in a bedroom. We would make out in the rest of the house, but in the bedroom we did not touch at all. We listened to music. We talked. We read magazines. We laughed at bad jokes. We did not touch, not in the bedroom, not until my 15th birthday.

When he opened the bedroom door, I saw candles, and Jordan turned on the bedroom stereo located between the door and the side of his bed. The sound of Whitney Houston, kind of soft not too much volume, came from the speakers. I gave him that tape. It was her first album, and it sounded completely sexy to me, and that was the album he was playing for us. On the nightstand, I saw a collection of condoms and lubricant that made my heart leap into my chest. Jordan pulled me close to him for another sweet series of kisses. As our lips parted, he said, "I'm ready for you if you're ready for me," and kissed me again before I could respond.

As our lips parted again, I told him I was ready, "But I don't really know what to do."

He kissed me again, and when our lips parted, he said, "That's okay, I've been studying and we'll figure it out together."

A few minutes or hours later, I honestly could not tell, Jordan and I were cuddled up together in his bed. I couldn't move. I couldn't speak. I'm not even sure if I was breathing to tell you the truth. I just stared at him, and thought about how beautiful he was in the candlelight. He opened the window above his bed. He pulled my head onto his chest, and lit a cigarette. After he took a puff, I asked if I could have one and he handed his to me. I sat there in bed and smoked my first half a cigarette in the arms of my first love feeling like I found that elusive heaven people at church were always talking about.

CHAPTER 21

I carried that night around with me the following year. I kept re-living our first time together in my head over and over again the same way someone might watch their favorite movie or listen to their favorite song. The first year of high school ended, the second year began, the days kept passing, but all I really remember from that year was how it felt each time Jordan and I were together. It seemed like everything was finally starting to make sense or come together.

The first year of high school ended without much notice. Jordan and I spent a lot of time together. Jordan and Zach spent a lot of time together. Abs and I spent a lot of time together. The four of us spent a lot of time together. We would talk about new subjects, try new books, listen to new music, and just spend afternoons roaming around, cutting up, and being young and somewhat free. In South Carolina at the time, 15 was the age where most kids started driving, and we were no exception. We poured over the manuals for our driving tests, and thought about all the places we would go. We dreamed of open roads, big cities – hell even Augusta, the city across the river, seemed huge at the time – and planned road trips we never ended up actually taking but outlined in exquisite detail all the same.

We were going to ride out to Waynesboro for the Bird Dog Festival, go out to a little town called Queens that apparently had a great diner that had been there forever like the one near our church, and visit every other little small town we could think of on our way to big cities and bright lights. We were going to go check out the little neighborhoods in Clearwater where Abs' family came from originally. We were going to drive out to the old fashioned drive thru place we heard about over in North Augusta, and the little pool hall in Edgefield that had been used in some movie. We wanted to see everything there was to see in the little towns that surrounded our own, and we even made plans to save up cash so we could check out New Orleans, Florida, or that place in Northern Alabama where all those 70s rock and soul artists made their records. We just dreamed the way you do when you're in high school and everything seems okay for a little while, when it seems like every day you might go somewhere new, see something else, and try out something special.

Zach was the first one to drive. His dad got a beat up, 1973, green truck – we think it was a Ford, but we were never really sure since it had been worked on so much over the years – and let Zach just run wild with the thing. Since his dad always seemed angry with him, we were surprised at the present. When we asked Zach about it, he just kind of got quiet, made a joke, and as was often the case, left the question unanswered. He just did not seem to ever talk much about his family, and we figured that was just his way. At the time, Zach was still 15, but he was approaching 16. Fifteen-year-olds were allowed to get what was called a restricted license that allowed them to drive during daylight hours unsupervised, but sixteen-year-olds who did not kill anyone while they were fifteen – or at least those who did not get caught doing so – could get a full license and disappear forever as far as anyone at the motor vehicles department was concerned. Although it took him three tries, Zach passed the road test, and began to terrify everyone with his driving ability.

The written test was basically a joke because the old lady that administered it did not pay attention. Most kids just walked in with the manual in their pocket or book bag to answer the multiple choice questions. It was hard to find anyone who did not pass the written exam with a perfect score. Jordan, Abs, and I took ours together not long after Zach. Jordan could have taken it much sooner – he was, after all, so much older than us – but he had no prospects for a car and his mom was scared of "Those crazy teenagers driving all this way and that, good Lord," so he put it off until Abs and I went to the place. The driving test was actually just as easy as the written test because all you had to do was kind of try and the guy doing the test really didn't care as long as you did not argue with him about politics like Zach did the first two times. He would tell you to just not give him any reason to worry, and he would let you go. He would then curse about government regulation and the sorry state of our liberal country the whole way through the driving test and attempt to explain why no government was better than the commies in Washington. Abs got her license without doing a three point turn, I got out of parallel parking, and we saw no reason to argue.

Armed with licenses, we spent most of that year parked in quiet locations where no adults would find us, riding over to the city across the river to go to the bigger record and magazine shops, and hanging out in parking lots with other teenagers. We would ride out to the lake to sit by the water, swim, or just drive around. We would go out to an abandoned racetrack out near the lake, and have fake races, drink beers, and smoke way too many cigarettes. On weekends and during the summer, we would sometimes pile into a car and head down to Charleston or Hilton Head for a day at the beach. The road was ours, and we made full use of it and the incredibly cheap – especially compared to now – gas prices. We would do odd jobs, gather up change from anywhere we could, and sell our possessions just to get back out on the road.

During our sophomore year, Abs got a car so she could drive to school, and began to rival Zach in terms of taxi services. Zach was still out of the loop about Jordan and I so Abs' car became a much more interesting option for us. We began funding her gasoline needs, and she would take us to movies, ball games, and stores. Abs especially enjoyed making sure she did not have to pay for any of these things, and we especially enjoyed the ability to be ourselves in the back of the car. We also helped her afford to take Simon to the Carolina Gamecocks stadium in Columbia because he always dreamed about it, she wanted to make him happy, and she felt a little guilty that she still had sex with Zach even though each time was definitely the last time. She brought back all these pictures of Columbia, and Jordan decided we needed to check it out someday.

On my sixteenth birthday, a year after Jordan and I spent the night together for the first time, I got a car. It was nothing to write home about, but it had four wheels, a working cassette player, and air conditioning that occasionally worked well. A soft green Toyota built in the 1980s, it was actually newer than a lot of the cars driven by the other kids in the neighborhood, and I fell in love with it right away. My parents gave it to me because they said I earned it with all the years I spent doing yard work and other odd jobs around the neighborhood. They said that stuff showed them I was responsible, and gave me a long talk about safety, car mechanics, and being careful on the roads.

Then they made me promise – or lie – that I would not drive too far from town, and I think we all knew not to put too much stock in that agreement, but I never checked just in case.

The first night I had a car, I took Abs and Zach and Jordan out to a basketball game. Zach had been drooling over the star forward on the college's team ever since she beat him down on the playground by his school. With my birthday cash, I got us all tickets for the night's game so Zach could see what she could do in a real game. The game was between the college in the city across the river and another college in southern Georgia. It was amazing to watch older kids play with such precision and tenacity, but at the same time, it was tremendous fun to listen to Zach's basketball mixed with sexual play-by-play of the action. We enjoyed the game that night, and sat out in the parking lot of the college after the game talking about what we would do if any of us ever went to college. Abs was sure she was going to be a doctor, and Zach thought college was for suckers who couldn't cut it in the military, but more than anything, he said he just wanted to get as far away from here as possible. Jordan thought it would be fun to be a teacher, and I kind of wanted to go into fashion, but I didn't feel comfortable saying that to them so instead, I said I wanted to maybe be a writer or something.

"What would you write about," Abs asked between puffs on a cigarette. We were sipping wine out of red plastic cups and sitting around the car. Everyone turned in my direction.

"I don't know," I said and I realized it was the truth, "Maybe what growing up was like with you lunatics."

Everyone laughed for a few minutes, and Zach asked, "Man why would you want to be a teacher? Aren't you ready to get the hell out of school?"

Jordan blushed a little bit, and said, "I don't know, I want to do something good for people, and I feel like the good teachers I have had were really important. I don't know, I just always thought it might be fun to introduce whole new generations to history or music or life skills, you know, something like that."

"What's so great about the military Zach," Abs asked.

"Its freedom babe, it's a way to go all over the world and get paid. You get to travel and do all kinds of cool shit. You get to get the hell out of town right away, and they pay for that shit. My cousin just enlisted, and he is going to get to play with all these guns and make good money working on the machines they use when we go fight. The thing is, no one touches you, you know, messes with you at all if you're a hard ass soldier. You're basically like invincible and get to see the world. I just think it sounds more fun than civilian stuff, more real you know, and it's the best way to get out of here fast, you know, gone, free, don't look back and all that shit."

"Civilian stuff," Jordan asks.

"Yeah, its just lingo, the military is like its own world man."

"What's the big deal about getting out of here," Jordan asks, and I'm reminded that Jordan actually sometimes thinks he might stay here. I don't like those times.

Zach looks down at his feet, and says, "I don't know man, I feel like it just has to be better somewhere else, you know, it has to better than this shit." He goes quiet, and doesn't elaborate, but instead, after a few seconds, he asks, "Are you going to save the world Dr. Abs."

Laughing, Abs says, "Hell no. I want to be a doctor because they get paid a ton of money, get a ton of respect, and can do whatever they want." Chuckling between puffs, she says, "But really I just think the body is so freakin' cool and I want to be able to play with it. I got this anatomy book at the book store here on campus, and I just thought about, you know, all the different things you could do with the body and all the ways it can be taken apart and put back together like a puzzle, you know. That's what I want to do."

"So I think what we've learned tonight," I say lighting a smoke and giggling a little bit, "Is that we need to be careful around Zach and Abs in the future because he might be playing with guns and she might be looking to take our bodies apart."

Laughing, Abs says, "Yeah and you can write a story about me cutting up bodies and Zach shooting up some town, and then Jordan can teach it to the kids," and we all just laugh for a few minutes in the parking garage free from the concerns of the rest of the world for just a few moments. We hear the sounds of other people partying outside the garage, we feel the cool breeze that flows through the night, and like so many other teenagers in so many other places we dream about futures that seem so far away.

After topping off his cup, Jordan says, "I guess we're out of wine," and turns the bottle upside down. It's another one from his mother's collection, another one emptied in the service of dissipating childhood, and it's almost a little sad to see it empty that night. We stay in the garage talking, smoking, laughing, and dreaming for about another hour. The first half of high school is almost over, but the future seems bright.

CHAPTER 22

By the time our sophomore year ended, nights where the four of us laughed together under the moonlight had begun to become less common. As the rest of the spring passed, we all started exploring new terrains that lessened our time together as a unit. I don't remember anyone explicitly requesting this shift, and I don't know if I really noticed it at the time, but it happened nonetheless, almost as if beyond our control. The four of us still came together from time to time, but the entrance of cars into our lives created other opportunities in other places with other people.

Best I can tell, the process began about a month after that basketball game when Jordan went to visit Roger, Abs got invited to attend an upcoming summer program in the arts, Zach met a woman named Willow that worked at a diner over in Augusta, and I found myself hanging out with a person from my past who suddenly re-entered my life in an unexpected way. In my case, I was looking through fashion magazines one day in the big bookstore on the south side of Augusta – their magazine section was almost as big as the whole store in my neighborhood – when a boy who looked somewhat familiar asked if he could get to the magazine rack below the one I was looking at. I moved out of the way, and he grabbed a couple magazines from the music section, and said thanks.

I felt like I'd seen him somewhere before, so I said so, and he just started laughing. "We went to elementary school together," he said before adding, "But I looked a lot different back then." As he started to leave, it hit me like a bolt of lightning, "Nicki," I asked thinking about the little tomboy that was always playing basketball during recess. Nicki had basically been one of the boys even back then, but now he, she, I wasn't sure honestly, looked even more like one of the guys. Nicki's parents moved in the middle of my third grade year – she was a fifth grader at the time or maybe he was – but I don't think any of us ever saw or heard about Nicki again after that. I tried in vain to remember more, but that was all I had.

"Well, its Nick now," he said, I would later learn that "he" was how Nick preferred to be addressed, "But yeah, that was me."

"Oh, I'm sorry Nick, I didn't know you changed your name. How have you been?"

With that question, a weekly ritual was established that would continue throughout the spring. Nick and I would meet at the bookstore, talk about all that changed since we were kids, and what it was like to change from Nicki to Nick. Nick's parents were not very happy with this change, but they gave up fighting it after his first year of high school. The house had become a kind of "don't ask don't tell" zone since then, and Nick was desperate to get out. After he graduated at the end of the semester, he was planning to move to Atlanta and continue his transition. There was apparently a lot more to a transition like that than I ever imagined all the days I thought about becoming a girl, and I was fascinated by Nick's knowledge of it. I introduced him to Lena by way of the phone, and Lena began helping him plan his move. Lena was also graduating, and planning to live on her own in the summer, so her and her friends helped Nick find places that were safe to live and potential places he could work.

As the weeks went by, I also learned that Nick had always been attracted to boys, girls, and what Nick called "Trans people." Nick explained that trans people were people like him who wanted to change their sex and people like me who crossdressed and there were a bunch of other kinds too. Nick also had to explain the term crossdressing to me. I realized how little I knew over and over again hanging out with Nick, and met a lot of other people who liked multiple sexes in a romantic way, and did not fit neatly into boy or girl only ideas. I would go back to Jordan and Abs with new stories, new people, and new terms that applied to people like me, and I felt much less alone than I ever had before that spring and summer. It was like a whole new world was opening up right in front of me.

I wasn't the only one learning more about myself. Jordan met up with Roger one day just to check in on him, see how he was feeling, and help him pack up some of the things in the house he no longer wanted to keep. Roger kept talking about maybe moving on from our little town, but he wasn't sure because he had a family here. I was vaguely aware of the family stuff, but I had never met them. While Jordan was at Roger's house that day, he stumbled across a flyer for a gay church that operated in Augusta, and asked Roger about it. Unlike me, Jordan still held out hope that one day he would be welcomed in church, and he still believed there was a higher power out there somewhere that cared about him. Roger was still a practicing Christian too. I didn't understand how they could still believe those old fairytales after all we had seen, but I respected their desire to remain religious and helped Jordan how I could. Roger told him about the church, which he and Daniel had been members of in the past, and suggested he check it out if he was interested.

One weekend in early March, Jordan did just that. Since he still did not have a car, I drove him to the church that Sunday morning, and stayed with him for the service. Partly, I did this to make sure he got to go, but another part of me did not trust anything with the word church in it and wanted to make sure he was safe. We arrived at the space just before the worship service began, and we were shocked to see men holding hands with men in a room decorated with crosses and Bibles. Even as someone who was already embracing a nonreligious life, I gotta admit it was an inspirational sight. For Jordan, it was the "promised land." He just stared open mouthed at the rainbows, the couples, and the cross like a child first entering a candy store. We took our seats, and enjoyed a surprisingly – for me – pleasant service.

Rather than damnation or sin, the focus of the service was love, hope, and embracing ourselves as creations of God who deserved love and care. It was almost completely opposite of any message I heard about people like us in any church at that point. The church also hosted support groups for people struggling with reconciling their sexuality and their faith, and Jordan signed up for one of these after asking if I could drive him to the meetings. Throughout the rest of the spring, Abs or I would take Jordan to the meetings, and to some of the worship services and social events put on by the church. When summer arrived and Jordan finally got a car, he began spending a lot of his time with the people at the church. Sometimes I would go with him, but mostly, he was on his own, finding his religion, and soaking up the company of others like him who wanted to be both gay and Godly.

While Jordan and I were "Finding our people," as he liked to say, Abs was finding her future, though she didn't know that at the time.

At the time, all she knew was that one of her poems had been selected for an award, and part of the award included a spot in a summer camp for emerging artists hosted in Charlotte, North Carolina. A few years later, participation in this camp would be one of the driving factors in Abs' admission to a liberal arts school, and years beyond that, she would cite that summer as the turning point that led to her scholarly career and accomplishments. At the time, she just wanted to spend some time away from our town after Simon had, finally learning about her and Zach's always the last time engagements over the years, broken off their relationship.

When Abs got the letter about the award in early April, she went into overdrive carrying a sketchpad and a journal everywhere. While we saw her from time to time when her and I met at the river or when she gave Jordan rides to church, she spent most of her time alone with her notebooks. Since I was going to the bookstore almost every week, she made a list of books she wanted to read, and I would pick up one or two each week. She would take it, read it, and then scribble notes all over it in the next week, and be ready for the next books. Some of the books were novels and collections of poetry, but others were about mathematics, anatomy, chemistry, and other subjects that seemed kind of surprising to me at the time. In classic Abs style, she downplayed all this work, and said she was only getting ready to show up all the real artists at the camp for fun.

No matter what she said, we could tell she was really getting into it. Her parents finally stopped fighting her about smoking earlier that year, and so she set up a kind of office on her back deck. We would come by to see her surrounded by books and notepads, a full ashtray, empty cups, and pens of various colors. She also began practicing what she called readings where sometimes Jordan, sometimes me, sometimes Zach, and sometimes all of us would become the audience and she would read her work in progress to us. We would ask questions, offer comments, and otherwise react to the poems and story segments and she would take notes on what we said or did. She got this idea from a book I picked up for her that was not on her list, but was on clearance. The book promised to provide emerging writers with tips of the trade so I thought she might like it. Apparently, she did. She worked through every exercise in that book, and then left us for the artistic camp in early June.

As the rest of us peeled off from the group one by one that spring, Zach seemed to get annoyed. Initially, he told Jordan and I that Simon breaking up with Abs was actually a plan for them to finally be together. When Abs showed no interest in this outcome despite continuing to sleep with him for the last time again and again, he explained to us that he lost interest in Abs, and that we should spend the spring and summer doing guy things although he still jumped each time Abs wanted to "hang out" for the last time. Unfortunately, Jordan was already doing guy things of his own getting to know his God, other gay men, and my body in ways that Zach did not know about, and we still did not think telling Zach about either of us was the smartest move. At the same time, I was drifting more and more away from guy stuff, and spending most of my time around other bisexual and trans – two new words I learned that spring – people over in Augusta. Neither of us were able to come up with good ways to explain this to Zach so instead Jordan said he was getting involved with his church and I said I was in a book club – neither activity likely to get much interest from Zach.

Things continued to be tense between the three of us – and Zach continued to basically avoid Abs except at each last time – until early May. One day, annoyed with us and looking for something new, Zach went into a diner in the city thinking maybe he would just get a job when he met a waitress named Willow. Four hours later, Willow got off work, and they went back to her place to have some drinks and try some cocaine she got from the cook at the diner. That night lasted two weeks, and we finally saw Zach again near the end of May when he showed up at Abs' final reading exercise in her back yard. His parents barely noticed he was gone, but we were all a bit concerned. Zach didn't care, and left once again annoyed.

Throughout the summer, Zach and Willow practically lived together doing drugs, doing each other, and doing work at the diner. Zach became a cook for the place, and Willow continued waiting tables. Zach was almost never home, and we barely ever saw him. He went with the crew of the diner when they had parties, and Willow got him into clubs as her guest. Willow was 22, and everything an-about-to-be-seventeen-year-old Zach could ask for in a fantasy. She had been a military brat as she put it when Jordan and I finally met her one night when we visited the diner just to make sure Zach was alive, and because – surprisingly, for me, I admit – we kind of missed the guy. She was tall, slender, and very sexual with everyone who moved in her field of vision – kind of like Zach actually. She finished high school out near Orangeburg, South Carolina, a little stretch of nothing that made even our little town look like a metropolis, and came to Augusta to be discovered as a singer or an actress or both. Zach was obviously high on something, and Jordan was really starting to get worried about him. Zach didn't care, and said staying with Willow was good for him. Willow sometimes sang in the karaoke bars and at open mic nights, but mostly she waited tables, did drugs, sold some drugs, and partied.

Throughout the summer, I noticed that I didn't see Jordan as much when he became more and more active in the church, and it bothered me a lot. At the same time, whenever I brought it up, Jordan would point out that I had new friends too and that neither of us were around as much as we used to be. Rather than fight, we let the topic rest. At the same time, though in a different way, I noticed the absence of Abs all summer, and I greedily devoured the couple of letters I got from her while she was gone. I also spent hours crafting my own letters to her. I wanted her to come home so bad, but I also knew the camp seemed to be the best thing for her. When it came to Zach, though, I noticed he was gone, but for whatever reason, it didn't bother me nearly as much as the absence of the other two.

Looking back, I think I only saw him three more times that summer after the night Jordan and I visited the diner. I know him and Jordan saw each other more because they had basketball summer practice in July, but I don't remember hearing anything about those practices that sticks out in my head. I also know that he got really drunk one night, and called the camp in Charlotte looking for – and cursing about – Abs, but I don't remember what else happened in that case, and I don't think I ever heard him or Abs mention it later. Times were changing, we were growing up, and moving in separate directions felt natural at the time, but when I look back, I wonder if something important got missed that summer.

CHAPTER 23

"I think I might be bisexual too," Abs says out of nowhere as we sit with Nick and his friend Rachel outside the big bookstore.

Abs had just returned home from her camp, and spent the entire ride over to the bookstore filling me in on the beautiful arts people created, the fun times singing around the campfire, the goofy little old guy at the store near camp that flirted with all of them when they went to get cigarettes or candy, the sounds of instruments waking her up each morning, the make out sessions that populated the camp's nighttime hours, and the hours she spent sitting by the water writing a story about a girl who becomes a dragon and saves the world from Republicans. She did not, however, mention this.

"Welcome to the club," Rachel says with a smile.

Rachel goes to the local college, and is studying to be a nurse. She fell in love with Nick years ago for "Exactly two weeks" before deciding Nick was the "Best friend ever I would not want to have sex with." Rachel also goes to Jordan's church sometimes, but she has had problems there with lesbian and gay people who don't believe bisexuality is real. I don't really understand this, and I haven't seen it myself at that point, but it seems to bother her a lot. Nick introduced us as part of his preparation for leaving town so I would have someone local to talk to, and we hit it off almost immediately. In fact, in the moment, I think that, with Abs, Rachel might become the "Best friend ever I would not want to have sex with." I am wrong and will only see Rachel a couple more times after Nick leaves. It's funny how often we guess wrong about people, and think they might be more or less important than they ultimately are.

"Where did that come from," I ask with a smile and softly grab Abs' hand.

Abs got home from camp this morning, and the first thing she did was come over to my house squealing, hugging, and laughing. I was squealing too. After our embrace, I said I was supposed to meet up with Nick and Rachel, but I could cancel. Instead, Abs suggested she come with me to see them. I loved this option, and we jumped in the car and headed out to the bookstore. Now, I was pretty sure this topic was why Abs wanted to hang out with the three of us today.

"There was this girl at camp. She was like us," Abs says pointing her finger back and forth between me and her, "She, you know, dressed in men's and women's clothing, you know." Taking a sip of her coffee, Abs continues, "But she also thought she might be like you," she points at Nick, "You know, she might want to become a boy at some point but she wasn't sure so for now she still wanted to be a she, you know." The rest of us nod, I squeeze her hand, and Abs says, "I just kind of fell in love with her, you know, and at first, it was no big deal because, you know, I thought she was just another guy, you know, but she was a girl who looks like a guy, and I liked that so maybe, you know, maybe I like more than just boys too."

As Abs spoke, her voice got softer and softer, and as she said the words "More than just boys too" Nick and Rachel reached across the table and all of us were now holding her hands and smiling at her. She looked up and smiled at the three of us, a little blush dissipating across her cheeks as her smile grew. Nick finally spoke after a couple minutes, "That sounds beautiful Abs, and whether or not you like more than just boys or just this one girl, we are here for you." All of us nod, and I take a mental note of the way Nick handles this situation. "Would you like to tell us about her?"

Abs smiles, and says, "She was amazing in every way. She was funny, smart, and beautiful, you know, like really beautiful. She looked like a younger Jordan Knight, you know, just wow, and she had this soft but strong voice. She is a painter, you know, she paints these pictures of women's bodies where certain parts of the body are blown up bigger for effect. She is really talented, and she wrote me a little poem about halfway through camp because she said I was cute for a straight girl, you know, but I read that poem thinking I don't want to be a straight girl, you know, and I don't know, you know, I really like her. She is just so cool, you know, very boyish like me but even boyish in like appearance or whatever, you know, but even more, and also like a beautiful woman too, like at the same time, you know. The only time I felt this way before was with Simon, you know, other people, you know, I might find them attractive, but that's about it, but with her and Simon, there is more to it I guess."

CHAPTER 24

A few nights later, I was lying in Jordan's lap in his living room while his mom was at work. It was the Saturday night before the first day of junior year. We were relaxing and saying goodbye to the summer. There was a party going on at the Thompsons and another couple parties over in the city where our newer friends were, but we just wanted some time alone.

We had already talked about the coming school year, the latest happenings at his church, my feelings about Nick moving to Atlanta, and his mom's new boyfriend who smelled like he lived in a liquor factory when I said, "Abs thinks she might be bisexual."

Jordan nodded, and said, "How did that happen?"

"She met an amazing girl at camp, developed a crush on her, and started thinking that maybe she could love more than just boys."

"I hope she doesn't tell Zach that."

"Zach," I ask, "Why would she tell Zach that, and why would he care now that he has Willow?"

"Zach and Willow broke up. She met some dude from Tennessee who is going to make her a star or something. Anyhow, Willow is gone. But Zach is still pretty hung up on Abs, he'd never admit it or talk about anything personal without jokes, but I can tell he loves her. Honestly, I think it scares him that he cares about her so much. I think Willow may have just been him trying to avoid that fact for a while. We were playing ball the other day, and he asked me if Abs was back in town, I didn't know and said so, but then he started going on and on joking – but maybe not really joking – about this is the year the two of them will get it right."

"What does that have to do with Abs maybe being bisexual?"

"Shit mate, you've seen how Zach reacts when he loses Abs to other guys, you really think he'd be able to handle losing her to a girl? This is Zach we're talking about. He still flinches when people even mention same-sex contact, and emotions seem to mess him up faster than any player on a basketball court."

"Good point," I say, though I don't really understand the difference. I do, however, realize that Zach doesn't have the highest opinion of women in the first place, and does get very upset whenever Abs hangs out with other guys. He seems to especially detest his mom, but I've only seen her a couple times so I have no clue what that's about. "I doubt she would tell him anyway, I think she actually is done with him at this point." Once again, I am wrong.

"I don't look forward to the day he knows that," Jordan says and starts laughing. He takes a sip of his soda, runs his hands through my hair, and says, "So, do you think she really is bisexual or is it just another thing Abs is trying out?"

I don't know why, but the question felt offensive to me. Something about the word "really" reminded me of Rachel's experiences at Jordan's church, but this was Jordan, he couldn't think like that, so I let it go. "I think that's something only Abs can answer," I said trying to figure out why his question bothered me so much. Something about it just felt, I don't know, mean or wrong. I would come across similar phrases many times in later years, and they always struck me in a negative way. It always felt like someone who didn't feel the way I did was seeking to place me in a box that made sense to them, and I always felt somehow erased. I didn't even have enough experience at that point to vocalize this feeling, but I knew it didn't feel right and I especially didn't like it from Jordan.

"That makes sense," he says, and smiles down at me. "Did you know Zach got a gun?"

"A gun," I ask a little scared at the thought of Zach with firepower. An image of Zach dressed like Rambo laying waste to a whole country flooded my brain.

"Yeah, it's a little handgun, he showed it to us after practice the other day. He said his cousin gave it to him for doing better in school this year. It was pretty cool looking, and Zach is going to take the team out to the shooting range to show us what it can do."

"A gun, really Bubba, you're going to a shooting range?"

"Shut up," he says laughing and tickling me, "I'm not saying I like guns or anything, but it could be fun to shoot one at a target."

"I reckin' it could Bubba, yep, I reckin' so."

Laughing, he says, "You're such an ass," and we both start laughing as I continue to talk in an overly Southern accent about babies and trucks and guns until he finally pins me on the floor and kisses me. "I love you even with your funny talking," he says in his own overly Southern accent and smiles at me.

"Well, I do declare," I say adopting my best Southern Belle impression, "What shall I do with such a big strapping man," before we both fall all over ourselves laughing.

CHAPTER 25

At the end of the first week of school, I took my first solo road trip since gaining my full license. It was Labor Day Weekend, and I didn't want the summer to end yet so I decided to go hang out with Lena and Nick in Atlanta. I had only been to Atlanta one time in my life, and I barely remembered anything about it. When I was much younger, my parents took me out to the city to see a Braves game at Fulton County Stadium, and all I really remembered about Atlanta was that it looked bigger than anything I ever imagined growing up in my tiny little town. I didn't know what to expect, but in some ways, that was kind of the point of the trip in the first place. I wanted another adventure before settling back into school.

"Why are you going to Atlanta," Jordan asked before I left.

"I told you, I want to get out of this town before school really gets going, and I want to see Lena's place. What's the big deal?"

Jordan was unhappy about my trip, but I had no clue why. "I don't know, I just thought maybe we could hang out this weekend."

"I thought you were going to be at the church all weekend."

"I am, but I thought maybe you could come with me." Jordan's church was doing some kind of special celebration that weekend, and there were events each day. I did not want to spend my holiday weekend in a church. I wanted to hit the open road, and relax before school got serious again. I also really wanted to see Lena and see the place Nick found where a lot of trans people – some like Nick, some more like me – congregated.

"No thank you, you enjoy the church, I'll hang out in Atlanta with Nick and Lena, and we'll spend all next weekend together."

Looking more annoyed than I expected, Jordan nodded, and I gave him a little kiss bye. I drove out of Jordan's neighborhood, and made my way to the Interstate. The Interstate that ran near our little town could take you to all kinds of places if you had a car, but I had never driven out of our little area except when I went over to Augusta, the couple times I drove over to North Augusta with Abs, and the time I went up to Aiken accidentally because I took a wrong turn.

I headed for Atlanta, and spent the next three hours driving past signs with the names of towns I had never heard of before, but was certain I would someday explore. Lena lived in an area of town that would become one of the hottest neighborhoods in the city in a few years. Her directions told me to get off of the Interstate at Moreland Avenue, and then weave through the neighborhood to an apartment building located behind a thrift store specializing in used clothes. I arrived at Lena's place around 10 o'clock Saturday morning, and parked in the area she told me about.

After I got out of my car, I stared at my surroundings for a little while. Atlanta was huge so that part of my memory was correct, but nestled here in this little neighborhood it also felt very comfortable. I saw people of varied ages, races, clothing styles, and accents walking around the neighborhood, and somehow felt at home. It was peaceful for me to stand in a city where almost no one knew who I was. There was a sense of freedom there, a feeling that I could do anything then just as quickly disappear back into obscurity. The people walking around barely seemed to notice me, and something about that made me feel very happy.

As I stood there looking around at all the people, I heard a familiar phrase, "Look at that silly boy." I scanned the area around me trying to find Lena, but I couldn't until I heard her say, "Look up silly," and there she was on the balcony of what I assumed was her apartment a couple stories above me. "Come on up," she yelled, and I began grabbing my stuff and heading for her building. I only brought a few items of clothing with me since I was only going to be there a couple days. I walked across the street, hit the buzzer on her door, and witnessed the building's front door open as if by magic.

When I reached the apartment, Lena hugged me with all her might and pulled me inside. Inside, I found what may have represented my own dream home at the time. It was just one room, but it had everything in it. Inside the door, you were against the far left wall, and Lena had a television and stereo set up on that wall with her Madonna poster set above both of these essential items. When I looked to the right, there was a little brown loveseat Lena said she got from a thrift store and a futon turned down into a bed against the far right wall.

There was a little coffee table in front of the futon, and a full ashtray beside a stack of books sitting there waiting for someone to remember them. Moving into the room, there was a small kitchenette along the far right wall, and Lena had put a little table with a coffee maker on it against the left wall. The back of the apartment had two closets opened to full view, and Lena's clothes hung there in all their majesty beside, on the right side, a door that led to the bathroom that only had a shower and no bathtub and on the left side, a door that led out onto the balcony. It was tiny. It was messy. It was dirty. It was cheap. It was heaven.

Lena led me out onto the balcony where we sat for the next few hours drinking coffee, smoking cigarettes and catching up. Her friend Greg lived next door with his current boyfriend, and they came out on the balcony for a while and delighted me with stories of life in the big city. We sat out there listening to chaos below, and laughing our way through my first day in the city. That night, Lena and I went roaming around looking at shops, empty storefronts, and bars filled with people. We went to a little park on the edge of the neighborhood, and sat down on a big rock. I was amazed by how quiet it could be nestled within such a big city.

As we made our way back to her apartment, Lena tugged on my arm and asked, "So what do you think of my city silly?"

Smiling, enjoying the feeling of her hand in mine again, I said, "I didn't know it was your city, how did that happen?"

Laughing, she said, "Always so silly."

"I love it here. It's like a whole different world, people just seem so different and nobody seems to bother all that much, its just, nice, I mean, I don't know, it feels more peaceful than back home."

"I knew you would like it. I love it here, and I'm never leaving, no more small towns for this lady, nope, I belong with the people," she says and starts dancing along the sidewalk. I watch her dance, and think about moving here myself after school.

When we get back to the house, Greg invites us over for some wine. The three of us – his boyfriend is at work – sit around talking about the city, my first day here, and our "lovers" as Greg calls them. Around 11 that night, I try to call Jordan, but he doesn't answer. About an hour later, we finish off the second bottle of wine, and I go back to

Lena's to sleep. I don't know how long they stay up talking, but when I leave they are deep in a heated debate about the best bars in the city and whether or not their neighborhood is cooler than some place called Buckhead. I don't realize it at first, but the door to the balcony in Lena's apartment is open when I take my spot on the loveseat. I think about closing it while I begin to fall asleep, but ultimately, I find the sounds from the street below soothing.

CHAPTER 26

I wake in the morning to the sound of car horns. Lena is on the futon sleeping, and I am still in the same spot on the loveseat wearing my clothes from the night before. The apartment smells like Jordan the night we first made love, like Lena's back porch after our first time – a sweet mixture of cigarettes and wine is the best way I've ever been able to describe the scent. It's a smell that will always make me think about my youth. I watch Lena sleep for a little while, and then I get up and get Lena's phone. I try to call Jordan, just to tell him good morning and that I miss him, but again there is no answer. I wonder what he's up to. I put the phone down, grab Lena's cigarettes because I am out, and make a cup of coffee. With these ingredients, I step out on the balcony to write in my journal.

I started keeping a journal over the summer because it seemed like doing so brought Abs a sense of peace. When I asked her about it, she said sometimes she just needed a space to let it all out, to freely vomit on the page. I liked this idea so I picked up a journal too. My journals are not like the ones Abs keeps. Abs writes about her own life and feelings, but for some reason, I mainly write fictionalized versions of my life and the lives of others. Something about writing these stories helps me deal with my actual life, but I'm not sure what that might be. I also don't keep my journals, but Abs does. Abs keeps them to refer to later, which I guess makes sense because it allows her to relive moments in her life. I throw mine away, and I don't really know why. I think I like the idea of setting the stories free once they are written, but that is only a guess. In any case, I spend the first morning I awake in a big city writing in my journal about a little girl who got lost in a big city only to be rescued by a kind gorilla who taught her the ways of the world.

I've been out on the balcony a couple hours and almost finished my gorilla story when Lena comes out wearing a t-shirt that drapes down to her knees and a pair of too cute pink panties that become visible when the wind moves her shirt. She sits down in the other chair and lights a cigarette. "How you doing silly?"

"I'm good. I like it here."

"Me too, well, I do once I wake up," she says puffing on her first smoke of the day. "Greg and I were up way too late with way too much wine that Greg was sure just had to get finished, my head hurts." I will always marvel at just how comfortable I felt that morning sitting on the balcony with Lena. I would return to Lena's various apartments in the coming years searching for that same comfort, but I didn't know that at the moment. All I knew was something about that city, that neighborhood, and that balcony spoke to me. Watching one of my oldest and best friends wake up, I wished Jordan could see the world outside our little town.

After three cigarettes, Lena said, "I really need a shower," and left the balcony. As she showered, I watched the drama unfolding on the street. People were setting up little stands to sell fruits and vegetables, and a group of kids were skateboarding across the street using the benches and signposts as accessories for their tricks. Over by the coffee shop on the corner, a guy who looked about my age was setting up a drum that he began to play and sing along to while people dropped money into the case at his feet. I was nestled in my own private space without anyone able to see me or bother me without at least looking up a bit, but I was surrounded by life and people. Something about that felt right.

A few hours later, both of us cleaned, awake, and filled full of coffee, Lena and I headed out to see the area where Nick was living. Lena and Nick struck up a bit of a friendship while they found Nick a place over the summer, and we were all supposed to meet at Nick's place first before going to a show. I didn't know it at the time, but my sixteen-year-old self was about to experience another couple of first times that would stick in my head forever.

We had to take the train to get to where Nick lived. I had never been on a train, but that wasn't the first I would remember most from this day. The train was nice though. It was kind of cool to just sit back and relax with Lena while we watched the city pass by, and the different people get on and off again as the train made its way to Nick's place. Lena was our navigator since I honestly had no clue where I was. The train worked with a semi-silent beauty that I still associate with the joy I felt flying through the city. I remember thinking it would take years to see every part of a city this size, and maybe that would be a fun project for me someday.

We finally got off the train at a station called East Point, and we stepped out onto a platform in the middle of two train tracks. Nick lived in an apartment in East Point, and the bar we were going to was in this area so we left the station and headed for Nick's place. East Point was a small town of sorts situated on the edge of Atlanta near where the airport clogged up traffic from all sides. When we got out of the station, there were people walking everywhere, but what caught my attention was how much like a tiny town the place looked. Without the train, I could have mistaken East Point for the little town I grew up in, and I found myself marveling at the difference between it and the center of the city where Lena lived. I must have stopped to stare or something because the next thing I remember is Lena grabbing my arm, and saying, "Come on silly."

When we arrive at Nick's place, Nick is sitting on the front stoop sipping a glass of wine and listening to music. Nick jumps up and gives us both big hugs before motioning for us to come inside. Inside, we find a one-bedroom apartment mostly populated by books and records. Nick puts his wine glass on the counter, grabs my hand, and pulls me toward the bedroom. Lena joins in pushing me from behind. I don't know what is happening, but I am certain I am being ambushed. When we enter the bedroom, I stop and just stare. On the bed, there are three skirts that look like they might be my size.

Smiling big, Nick says, "Tonight we're going to a drag show with lots of trans, gay, bi, lesbian, and crossdresser folks so we thought you might want to try out your dreams."

"I, uh, I, well, I, what do, uh, what should, I, uh, do," I stumble these words out of my mouth as I stare at the clothes in front of me. Do they really want me to wear these out in public tonight? Tonight? Am I ready for that? This is not my grandmother's back room. This is an actual bar with actual people who will actually see me. I'm shaking, but also kind of excited. I played out moments like this in my head so many times I lost count, but standing there, I realized I would never know unless I tried. I could run every possible scenario – many of them ended bad, I admit – but I had no way to know what it would feel like and how people would react. An internal debate that was all too familiar played out in my head.

"You don't have to do it if you don't want to silly," Lena says putting a hand on my back, "But if you do want to, we'll be there with you all night and you'll be safe at the club."

I look at each of their faces. They both smile at me, and I ask for a minute alone. As they leave the room, I find myself torn between fear and excitement just like I was the first time Jordan kissed me. I decide that I'm never going to have a more supportive chance to see what it feels like to dress how I want in public, and I remind myself that no one in this city that doesn't already love me knows me at all. With these thoughts repeating in my head, I pick the black skirt. I put it on slowly, and check myself in the mirror only about four thousand times more than I probably need to. I like the way it fits. I check it out one last time, and leave the bedroom.

They are waiting for me, and right away, both of them start squealing and run to hug me. We bounce up and down and laugh in the living room for a few minutes, three friends enjoying a dream come true, and Nick turns on some music. The living room becomes a dance party, and remains such for the next hour or so until Taylor arrives home from work. As Taylor and Nick go into the bedroom for Taylor to change and to have a couple minutes alone, Lena pulls me to the side and we slip outside to the front porch. Lena lights a smoke, smiles at me in a way that kind of lights up her eyes, and says, "Remember that day you were looking through my closet?"

Blushing more than I would like to admit, I nod, and she says, "You were looking at the clothes weren't you? It wasn't about sex at all, was it?"

"I thought you would think I was crazy. You already thought I was silly for falling in love with Jordan back then and I didn't really know how to talk about, well," I gesture to the skirt, "This. When you suggested another option, I chose that over the truth."

"I didn't take advantage of you that day did I," she asks looking down at the ground.

I reach out and raise her head so we are eye to eye, "No, you did not. You gave me a beautiful experience that day that I think I'll treasure forever. Now that I think about it, though, how did you know I liked girls' clothes? Did Nick tell you? Who else knows?" A bit of panic ran through my body at the thought that people could have figured me out. What if other people were figuring it out?

Lena started laughing. "We did good didn't we," she said, and then explained how she noticed that I was wearing panties when she was in town for Christmas. "You were bending over to get something, and the top of them became visible." I start to giggle, and she says, "Yes, I was checking out your butt, sue me," and sticks her tongue out at me. After having met people who crossdressed through Greg, her first thought was that I probably did too, but had not told her or anyone yet. "So, I got in touch with Abs and asked if she knew anyone who did that," and after learning that Abs did not know anyone who did, she figured I wasn't ready to tell people.

"Then, well, I was helping Nick unpack some boxes, and I saw a picture of you and Nick looking at skirts in a store," she said. I remembered Taylor taking the picture because she thought we were too cute. "So, I said what is this, and I could just tell by Nick's face that he knew so I told him I knew, but you probably didn't know I knew. At first, he felt really bad, but I think knowing that I thought it was good helped him feel better." She throws out her smoke and continues, "Anyway, so when you said you were coming to visit and wanted to go to the bar, we thought maybe we could try to surprise you. Nick told me about your dreams of dressing that way in public, and we thought, we can make that happen. We just wanted you to know that it's okay and we support you so we thought let's try."

I didn't know what to say, so I just hugged her, and while we were hugging Nick and Taylor came out ready for the bar. We went out together, and spent hours at the bar, but I barely remember any of the details. What stuck in my head was the way my friends created a chance for me to try out a long time dream, and the way I felt moving through that club in that skirt throughout the night. It was a blur. It was beautiful. It was freedom. I felt alive, and it was all thanks to these wonderful people and this wonderful city.

CHAPTER 27

"So did you sleep with Lena," Jordan asks as I walk up to his front porch Monday evening. We haven't spoken all weekend because he has not answered the phone, and I have just returned from Atlanta.

"What are you talking about," I sneer.

"Did you fuck Lena? You drove all the way to Atlanta to see her so I'm guessing you did."

"What the hell is wrong with you? I just got home, I come to see you, and that is the first thing you say to me after not answering the phone all weekend? No, I did not sleep with Lena, but now I kind of wish I had." I kind of wanted to strangle him.

"Whatever," Jordan says, and goes inside the house. I follow him inside and the smell of alcohol hits me hard. I think he's been drinking the whole time his mom's been at work.

"Hey, what is up with you?" He looks like he's seen a ghost. His hair is messy, I don't think he's bathed, and he stares at the floor.

"You really didn't sleep with her?" "Of course not, I'm with you for some reason I can't think of right now."

"But you wanted to sleep with her, didn't you?"

"What do you mean?"

"You're still attracted to her, you want to sleep with her again, exactly what I said."

"Of course I'm still attracted to her, but no I don't want to sleep with her again. I'm with you, ya jerk!"

"Then why did you go all the way to Atlanta to see her," he says getting up off the couch, and going to grab another beer. "Why would you drive all that way to see her and not have sex with her?"

"Because she's my friend you asshole! Where is this coming from? Are you taking some class on woman hating all the sudden!"

"You really didn't sleep with her?"

"I'm getting tired of this fucking question Jordan. No, I did not sleep with Lena, and I haven't slept with Lena or anyone else since you and I decided we were a couple. You know this already."

"Well, I have, so there's that."

I thought I was mad before, but after that, "What the FUCK DOES THAT MEAN JORDAN?"

"I had sex with Lenny."

"WHAT?" Lenny was one of the guys at the church. Jordan and Lenny had been hanging out for months, but this was the first time I heard anything like this. I wanted to kill Lenny. I wanted to kill Jordan. What was happening?

"Over the weekend, I don't know, Saturday night we were hanging out, nothing special, just hanging out after the church event. It was no big deal and you were gone, I don't know. I was kind of pissed at you for leaving, I guess, and we were drinking, I don't know, it just kind of happened. It just, no big deal, just, I don't know, just kind of happened before I thought about it, I figured you were with Lena anyway so what was the difference, I don't know."

"No big deal? FUCK YOU! You were pissed at me, well why not talk to me about it instead of cheating on me?"

He started to say something, but at that moment I just wanted to be anywhere other than his house so I headed out the door. If he followed, he was really slow because I got all the way back to my car, cranked it up, and drove off with the door to his house still standing open and empty. I didn't know where I was going, but I needed to get the hell away from him. He had slept with Lenny then accused me of sleeping around. What the hell was that? What was going on? I didn't know what to do, I wanted to break something, punch something, I just didn't know what to do. In the end, I did what I always did when the world stopped making sense. I went to find Abs.

CHAPTER 28

I could see Abs sitting on her front porch as I pulled into her driveway that night. I just sat in the car for a minute before getting out asking myself if this was really happening. I was planning to tell Jordan all about my night at the bar and how wonderful Atlanta would be for us when we finished school. I was planning on tasting the lips I'd spent all weekend missing, and listening to whatever the events at the church had been like. I was planning on a pleasant welcome home with the man I loved, and I got shit on instead.

As I approached her front porch, Abs said, "Well, I guess he told you at least. Good, if he had not, I was going to kick his ass."

With that, I just fell into her arms and started crying harder than I ever had before in my life. I felt like I was dying. Every part of my body seemed to hurt all at once, and I couldn't make it stop. My body was shaking, and I was vaguely aware of Abs telling me it would be okay, but I just wanted to crawl into some hole and cease to exist as soon as possible. I wanted to stop feeling, feelings suddenly sucked. I wanted a way to turn them off at least for a little while. Abs ran her hands through my hair, but all I could think about was the last time Jordan did that, before the weekend, before he cheated on me, before I felt like I did at that moment. I wailed into Abs' body like a newborn wishing for the pain to stop.

It didn't stop. It didn't stop for a long time. At some point, Abs took me inside and put me to bed on her couch. I didn't know it when I got there, but her parents were out of town and so it was just the two of us when I woke up in the morning and saw her sleeping on the other couch. She must have heard me stirring because she woke up too, and asked if I wanted a cup of coffee. I said yeah, and told her I wasn't going to school. She said she'd stay home with me, and we went out on the back porch. I lit a cigarette, stared out at the woods behind her house, the woods Jordan and I called home so many nights, and asked, "What is going on?"

"Jordan showed up here late Saturday night crying. Apparently he had sex with one of the boys at his church, and he felt horrible about

133

it. He was a mess babe, like totally messed up emotionally and a little bit drunk. He was babbling about Lena and Zach and bisexuality and all kinds of stuff, but he wasn't making much sense at first. He cried for a good while, and finally, when the tears subsided for a little while, he told me what happened."

"What happened?"

"So, you remember how Rachel said she ran into some crap at that church about bisexuals? Well, apparently Jordan ran into it too for dating you, you know. Some of the people there, including the one he slept with Saturday, don't believe in bisexuality. They think that it's just like a phase or something, you know, and that you can't trust people who are that way. They talk about how they've heard of bisexual people who all end up either really being gay or go back to straight people. Jordan, you know, well, he has apparently been hearing this stuff for months from a group of them."

"He never said anything to me about it."

"I figured as much. In classic Jordan style, he probably kept it all to himself. I'm guessing he defended you, you know, but by the time he came here Friday night they had him all but convinced that, you know, like it was just a matter of time before you cheated on him or just plain left him for a girl. He was terrified of it, he said, but he didn't know what to believe."

"He could have believed in me," I said tearing up again.

"I know. Hell, he could have talked to me about it, you know, but he didn't. Anyhow, the final straw came on Thursday afternoon. Jordan was at basketball practice, and he mentioned to Zach that you were going to Atlanta for the weekend. Zach, because he is Zach you know, interpreted this to mean you were going up there to "nail" Lena. Zach started going on and on about you and Lena getting it on in Atlanta. So, you know, Jordan said no you were just going to see your friends up there. Zach then explained to Jordan, in a way that makes me embarrassed to have slept with him mind you, that there was no way a guy would drive three hours to see a girl he was not having sex with. Apparently, Zach's false wisdom was the last straw for Jordan, and he left practice that day thinking you and Lena had something going on the side."

"He seemed aggravated with me Friday, and wanted me to stay and go to church with him, but he didn't tell me any of this."

"Well, Saturday, after you left, Jordan went to the church carnival thing, and he spent all day there with his church friends, you know, just hanging out. After the carnival, they all went out to this guy Ron's house, and got to, you know, drinking and making out and what not, you know, a regular party. Jordan was feeling lonely and was sure you were feeling Lena by this point so he just drank and felt like shit. Anyway, there was a guy there named Lenny who has apparently had a crush on Jordan for like months."

"What do you mean?"

"I'm not sure, but Jordan said Lenny had been interested in him and he just ignored it and told Lenny he had a boyfriend."

"He didn't tell me that either. I've met Lenny, but I never knew he had a thing for Jordan or that Jordan knew about it."

"Oh, well, that's what Jordan said. Anyway, so, you know, this guy Lenny is trying to cheer Jordan up, and they're drinking and hanging out at the party. Jordan said it just kind of happened, he didn't plan it, but they just started kissing and it went from there. Afterward, he felt like shit, and so he came here – don't worry I gave him hell for drinking and driving like an idiot. Anyhow, that's all I know. I told him he should talk to you, and he went home later that night once I could tell he was able to drive."

"Well, he talked to me alright. I got to his house last night after he had not answered the phone all weekend, and he accused me of sleeping with Lena and kept at it until I finally screamed at him."

"Really? Shit, I thought he would call you or just tell you what happened."

"Nope, though he seemed drunk yesterday too so he might have just gone home and went on a bender or something, but I doubt it since his mom would have probably noticed."

"Nope, she's out of town."

"What?"

"She left Saturday with that guy she's dating. They went up to the lake, not the big one over here but some little one over near Queens or Louisville."

"I didn't know that. So maybe he was on a bender, but he didn't tell me what happened until after I screamed at him, and all he told me was that he slept with Lenny and it was no big deal."

"I bet you wanted to kill him."

"You always were smart."

"I guess we're lucky Zach's the gun nut instead of you."

"Very lucky."

"Shit, this sucks."

"Yes it does. Hey, when you and Simon broke up, how long did it hurt like this for?"

"Sorry babe, it still does a little bit, and we didn't have near the history the two of you have. You might have to get used to the pain for a little while." As is often the case, Abs was right in this regard, but in the moment, I was really hoping she was wrong.

"Is there anything I can do?"

"Can you let me hang around here today until school is out, and I can go home? I really don't want to be around anyone else."

"You got it. What are you going to do about Jordan?"

"I really don't know. I don't know if we're together, broken up, both, I don't know anything right now. All I really know is whatever we are, it's on him to come talk to me." I lit another cigarette, and said, "I don't know. I guess I'll wait and see what happens next."

CHAPTER 29

What happened next was nothing. Over the next few months, I didn't see or hear from Jordan at all. He didn't call. He didn't send me any letters through Abs or anyone else. He didn't show up at my school. He just ceased to exist it seemed. I heard from Abs that he was alive at least. He was drinking too much, she said, and he was still going to the church, but she didn't hear from him much either. He called her occasionally, usually late at night after drinking it sounded like, asking how I was. I heard from Zach that he was still going to school. He was drinking more like a man, Zach said, and he was still hanging out in the city a lot. They still hung out before and after school. I didn't hear from him at all.

I did think about him a lot. In truth, I missed him more than I wanted to admit. I wanted him to call or write or something. Even on the days where I felt like I would have just cursed him out and maybe beat the shit out of him, I wanted him to call me. The first month I made sure to get home from school as fast as possible, and I stayed home mostly on the weekends in case he called. It was odd for me since I rarely spent much time at home. My parents kept asking why I wasn't going out anymore, but I didn't really have anything to tell them. I didn't have anything at all. I filled up three journals in that first month writing all kinds of other ways our fall could have gone, and smoked way too many cigarettes trying to figure out what happened. It still didn't make any sense to me. I wanted him to say something. I wanted him to apologize. More than anything, I still just wanted him, and I hated that fact more than anything I had ever disliked in my life.

At the same time, I was so angry with him that I thought I would break his face if I saw him. I couldn't believe he would do this to me, but my anger always turned quickly into sadness, loneliness, and thoughts about all the good times. If I closed my eyes and focused really hard, I could still feel the touch of his lips. I started drinking wine that I got from the place where we bought cigarettes, and smoking while I drained the glasses trying to recreate the smell of his skin, but it only made things worse because the smell also reminded me of Lena. More than anything, I just waited.

Abs would come by and check on me sometimes. Abs asked more than a few times if she needed to tell Jordan off, beat him up, or stop talking to him, but as much as I appreciated where she was coming from, none of these things would make me feel any better. In early December, three months to the day since I had last seen Jordan, the semester was coming to an end, and Abs showed up at my locker. "There is a party tonight out at Tommy's house, and I so so so think we should go to it, you know, to have some fun?"

Tommy was a senior known primarily for his parties. No one seemed to know if he actually had any parents, but if he did, no one had ever seen them. He lived in a huge house out on the river, at the end of a road in our neighborhood that only went to and from the river, and threw regular parties. The houses on the river made even the ones in the fancier neighborhoods look tiny. Abs and I had gone to one when we were in our first year of high school, and we still talked about it. It was like something out of one of those cheesy teenage movies that all had about the same storyline. There were people everywhere, drinking, making out, having sex, skinny dipping in the river, and just destroying the place. It was insane, but it was also a lot of fun. Abs had gone back many times since that first party, but I preferred much smaller events.

"I don't know if I'm up to partying just yet Abs."

"Look, sooner or later you have to start having some fun again. I know you don't feel like it, but I need a good wingman, so do it for me, please!"

"I don't know Abs, do you really need me there?"

"Yes, because otherwise I might spend the whole party worried about you. Would you want to ruin my fun? Plus, I slept with Zach again, and this time it is so the last time, which means I need to meet some new people like yesterday."

"You're full of shit, you know that?"

"Yes I do, so you gonna go with me, pretty please?"

"I guess so, but I might not stay too long."

"Stay as long as you want, but at least try to have some fun."

CHAPTER 30

When we arrived, we found people doing shots of some type of liquor they were happy to share in the driveway. Instead, we took beers out of the coolers sitting on the gaping front porch that spanned the front of the home. Tommy was at the door smiling and chatting with people as they arrived. He waved us in, and made sure we knew that the bedrooms on the third floor were off limits.

As we entered the foyer, we saw a staircase that led to the second floor. A handful of kids were already sitting on the stairs chatting, making out, and drinking. Abs wanted to survey the house so we went to the right where a living room that spanned the whole width of the house awaited our inspection. At the front of the room, a group of kids were playing with instruments, and setting up for a set. Some of them were quite talented and often played shows in the area and at other parties. Moving past the band, we saw both of the couches were full of what looked like a mixture of sophomores and seniors passing around a bong, some cigarettes, and a few beers. They offered us a hit, but we kept moving. In the back of the room, right beside the doors to the back deck area, a couple had taken hold of the loveseat, and already removed most of each other's clothing.

From here, we turned left and walked into the kitchen. A whole other gang of people from our junior class were passing around food, tapping kegs, and watching two senior girls dance topless on the kitchen table. Laughing, I said, "You want to join the show," and Abs giggled and said, "Nah, wouldn't want to make the other girls self conscious," as we stared out at the back deck where people were grilling hot dogs and others were having a make out session on the lounge chairs. Abs lit a cigarette, offered me one that I took and lit, and said, "Want to check out the rest of the place?" I nodded, and we followed the little hallway that curved to the left.

It was at this point that I noticed that part of dating someone from another school and having to keep that relationship a secret meant that I knew very few of the people at this party. Over and over again, people would stop and say hello to Abs, and ask her who her friend – me – was. Many of these faces looked familiar to me from classes and hallways, but I had never noticed just how little I socialized at school until that moment. I could not have named one tenth of the people there that night, and just as few seemed to know who I was. It was an odd feeling to realize that I had inadvertently become a stranger in my own school.

As we walked down the hallway, Abs told me that she made out in the kitchen one time at one of these parties. I nodded approvingly as she pulled the door to what looked like a bedroom open, and revealed a couple – temporary or lasting was hard to tell – in the middle of intercourse. Interestingly, they didn't seem to notice the intrusion, and we quickly went into the next door, which led to a garage filled with two beautiful cars. "Nothing to see here," we both said at the same time, and tried door number three, which was a staircase. With a giggle, Abs headed up the stairs and I followed her.

Upstairs, it was much quieter. We had probably not reached the point of the evening when people would start sorting out into the bedrooms contained on the second floor. We checked out each of the bedrooms – 6 of them for some reason – and enjoyed the privacy. When we got to the last one, we took seats on the bed, lit a couple cigarettes and toasted the evening. Since we were not supposed to go up to the third floor, it appeared Abs' ritual was over. Abs had always been fascinated by houses, and this was a kind of tour she did in almost every house she ever entered. Even in houses, like this one, she had been in before, she wasn't fully comfortable until she toured the whole layout. I always enjoyed these tours, and often, like that night, followed along. As we sat on the bed smoking, she said, "Okay, so I want to go be social, are you going to be okay?"

Smiling, and not only doing so to make her feel better, I said, "Yeah, I'll be good. Are you drinking tonight?" This was our long practiced conversation. We picked up beers we barely touched when we first got here, but if Abs was actually going to really drink I would stay as long as she did to keep an eye on her. If she wasn't drinking, then she would ask if I wanted to, and if I did, she would stay as long as I did to keep an eye on me. If neither of us were drinking, we were free to come and go as we pleased.

"Nope, are you?"

"Nope." Abs got up from the bed, disappeared into the hallway, and we lost sight of each other for the rest of the night.

The bedroom had a little fridge in it, and so I set my beer on the nightstand and checked to see what was in it. To my surprise, there were bottles of water and orange juice. I took one of each, and sat back on the bed. I don't really know how long I was sitting on the bed, but by the time I got up to use the restroom both of the bottles were empty, the house sounded much louder, and I was feeling tired. After using the restroom, I figured I should see what was going on in the rest of the house, and maybe head home for the night so I walked to the door, opened it, and stepped out into a hallway that was now crowded with people.

Before I took a second step, a blonde-haired girl who looked kind of familiar even though I doubt we had ever spoken grabbed me and said, "Oh my, you're the cutie that is always with Abs." "My" had extra syllables, Abs was drawn out quite a bit, and the whole sentence was slurred so I assumed the person had been drinking.

I started to say yes I am, but right as I got the "yes" out of my mouth, she put her tongue in it. I was surprised to say the least, though also flattered, as she pushed on my chest and the two of us ended up back in the bedroom. She kept kissing me and her hands dug into my sides like she was a wrestler or something. I remember wondering how someone so much smaller than me could grab me so hard. After a few seconds, I disentangled my body and mouth from hers, and backed away from her. She kind of slurred words that might have been, "What, don't you want it," before falling down on the floor and starting to giggle. For the first time since I last saw Jordan, I laughed for real at my location in this absurd moment. I dropped to one knee and let loose laughing so hard that I started to cry for a minute. As I did, she slid down on her side, made a grumbling noise that only made me laugh harder, and passed out.

From the research Abs and I did years before, I knew all too well that bad things could happen to people who passed out at parties, and how unlikely such people were to ever get justice in our system after such bad things happened so I picked her up off the floor. I made sure she was breathing, placed her in the bed making sure she was in a position where she could safely sleep it off, and headed for the room's exit. I locked the door behind me so no one could get in while she was vulnerable, and was about to make my way through the hallway to find Tommy – who had a reputation for protecting people and especially drunken girls at his parties ever since he beat the hell out of someone who took advantage of a girl– when someone grabbed my arm, and said, "Where is Charlotte?"

Stunned, I said, "Who is Charlotte?"

At this point, I learned that the girl who attacked me a moment ago was named Charlotte, and that this was a friend of hers who was her sober protector that night. Relieved that someone could look after Charlotte, I smiled big and explained that Charlotte was asleep in the bed in the room behind us, but before I could finish my sentence the friend slapped me so hard I felt my head rattle around for a few seconds. "What the hell lady," I said as she went past me and started trying to open the locked bedroom door.

At this point, Tommy showed up, and started speaking to the friend who smacked the shit out of me. Apparently, the friend left drunken and nearly passed out Charlotte on the second floor right before I came out of the bedroom so she could go get Tommy to help get her friend out to her car. She had then come back to find Charlotte gone, and seen me come out of the bedroom laughing. This did not look like a good situation to her, and I must admit I would have felt the same in her shoes. When I told her Charlotte was asleep in the bedroom with that big smile on my face, she thought I raped Charlotte so she smacked the shit out of me. I would have done the same to me in that situation, and I smiled again at my admiration of her. I heard all this as Tommy opened the door, and they found Charlotte safely passed out, untouched, and sleeping.

Having had enough drama for one night, I took this as my cue to go home. I slipped down the stairs, out the front door, and into the night. I lit a cigarette thinking about how much I admired the woman who smacked the shit out of me, and how it actually turned out to be a pretty good night. I started walking home, and figured that was the end of my evening. I was wrong yet again. This was becoming a recurring theme. Twenty minutes later as I walked the road that led back to my house, a car flashed it's lights, and then pulled up beside me. Sitting in the driver's seat was the lady who smacked the shit out of me, and she did not look happy.

"Hey," she said, her voice shaking a little bit. Okay, at least the unhappy look was no longer a sign of pending violence.

"Hi," I said, "Is your friend okay?"

"Yeah, uh, she's sleeping it off in the backseat. I'm going to take her home."

I looked in the back window, and sure enough, there was Charlotte. I was glad to see her safely out of the house. "Cool," I said and lit a smoke.

The woman put the car in park, and said, "Can we talk?"

"Sure," I said wondering what she wanted to talk about. "There is a parking lot, for the public swimming pool, just around the corner if you want to get out of the road." She nodded, and so did I. She drove around the corner, and I started walking again.

CHAPTER 31

When I caught up, she was standing beside the car smoking a cigarette. I had not noticed it before, but she was very pretty. She had a curvy frame with wide hips and pronounced breasts that was perfectly symmetrical from head to toe. She was wearing a pair of jeans, and a Pearl Jam t-shirt that fit well with her makeup and her light brown hair. I didn't think I had ever seen her before, but considering how few people I knew at the party, this did not surprise me. She was staring at me as I approached the car, and holding her cigarette in her left hand between two silver rings that looked like they could have been part of one of the sets Roger and the magazine store owner were always talking about when I was younger.

"Hey again," she said as I approached.

"Hi again," I said with a smile. "What's up?"

"Look," she said, "I'm sorry I hit you," and then she paused.

"I'm not," I said quickly in the midst of the pause.

"You're not," she said looking surprised.

"Your friend could have been hurt, raped even, and you were trying to protect her. Then you came up and saw some guy leaving a bedroom he said she was in, and thought the worst. I would have done the same thing so I see nothing you should apologize for."

"It happens a lot," she says softly kicking her feet together.

"Way too much," I say, and the sad part is we know we're both right. I learned about it when Abs had two different friends raped at parties, and we started looking into information on the topic. Most reports we could find suggested it was an incredibly common problem in our country, and that's why we came up with a system for watching each other's back whenever we were at parties, and tried to mainly attend parties where the host had a good reputation.

"Do you know someone it happened to?"

"I did, but she doesn't live around here anymore, and I haven't heard from her in a long time. She was friends with my friend Abs, and it was terrible."

"It is terrible." After she said these words, we just stood there for a few minutes looking at each other, looking at the ground, looking back at each other. We both knew what she just told me, and we both knew there was nothing I could say. She started rubbing her shoulders with her hands, and stared at me for a minute. "I'm Claire," she said softly, "Maybe I'll see you around sometime," and she got back in her car, put it in drive, and left the parking lot.

I stood there thinking about Claire for about five cigarettes worth of time. The sky was clear that night, and I kept looking up at the stars and thinking about the pain she must have been carrying inside her because of some asshole. I thought about how many Claires there were out there, and how I never seemed to hear about anyone doing anything to stop this stuff from happening. I thought about Charlotte, and hoped she knew how great it was to have a friend who would look after you and be there for you when it mattered. I thought about how much friends like that shape our lives whether or not we realize it at the time, and then, I went home.

CHAPTER 32

The next morning, I was sitting on my back porch when Abs came up the driveway. She was actually hopping for some reason. As she approached, I said, "So did you have tons of fun at the party?"

Smiling big, she said, "That house was awesome!" Sitting down beside me, she added, "I'm going to live in a place like that someday, wait and see." I asked her if she wanted a drink, and she asked if I had orange juice. I went inside and got her a glass of orange juice. When I came back, she said, "Where are your folks?"

"They went out to church, then the flea market, usual Sunday afternoon for as long as I can remember."

"Cool, what you up to?"

"Not much, I was writing about a girl I met last night."

"You met a girl?"

"Not like that, calm down tiger."

"Awe, well at least you went out. What was with the girl?"

"I don't know," I lied since I didn't want to give away her privacy especially if Abs knew her. Abs taught me a lot about this stuff when it happened to her friends, and one lesson she made clear was the importance of protecting the privacy of people. So, instead of telling her what I learned, I said, "She was just interesting to me, I kind of admired her and enjoyed talking to her."

"You ever seen her before?"

"I don't think so. Her name was Claire," and I described her.

"Oh, I know her," Abs said, and I thought, of course you do. You know everyone. "She's a senior, keeps to herself mostly, doesn't date that I know of, but really smart and sweet. She hangs out with a lot of the band kids at lunch, but I've never really seen her outside of school, you know. You interested in talking to her more?" It turned out she didn't date much because she was in one of the best long term relationships I have ever encountered with an older guy named Devin who I swear could have been a model.

"Maybe, if we run into each other, but probably not. I'm not really in a good place for thinking about other people right now."

"That makes sense. Speaking of other people, did you hear about what's his name?"

"What? No, what's going on?"

"He's back." My heart froze. When he had been sent away for "treatment" a couple years before, I felt bad for him, but I also felt scared because he knew about me, about the storeroom, about things I didn't want to become well known just yet.

"Oh," I said, trying to sound calm, "When did he get back?"

"Well, you remember his parents sent him to the religious nuts to fix his gayness, right? Well, you know, that didn't work, but anyhow, he was there for about six months, and then his parents put him in a Christian private school upstate for a while, but he didn't do so well there, and they were worried about him. Anyhow, you know, so he's back here now, and he's going to Jordan's school."

"Did Jordan tell you that?"

"No, he was at the party last night. I saw him and talked to him for a while. Don't worry, the storeroom didn't come up so I don't think he's planning to tell people about you. He did ask me if I still hung out with you and Jordan, and I said I did. That was it."

"Is he okay?"

"I don't know, you know, he was very timid, you know, like scared of his shadow. We talked for a few minutes, but then some people came over to say hey to me, and he just kind of slipped away. I didn't see him again after that."

"He said he's going to Jordan's school?"

"Yeah, he said he was going there starting in the spring. He lost a year when his parents sent him away so he's only a sophomore. His parents don't want him anywhere near public school because for some reason they decided that was how he got gay."

"I didn't know we had a course in that."

"Me neither."

"I could have learned so much."

"I know, right," she says and we both about fall over laughing. "Maybe that's how you ended up in between, you needed the course and they didn't let you take it. Anyway, he's going to be at school with Jordan and Zach and I guess he'll be back at church."

"No, his parents stopped going a while back. My mom said they are now going to the church that runs Jordan's school. I think they got it pretty hard, or felt like they did, from the other parents."

"Well, then I guess you might not even see him."

"I guess not. Works for me, though I do hope he's okay."

"I'm not sure how he could be after being sent away."

"Me neither, but I can hope."

CHAPTER 33

"Please tell me you are not as sad as you look right now," Claire says walking over to me in the bookstore in Augusta.

"Is it that obvious," I ask. I was thinking about Jordan. My birthday has come again, and it has been six months since I've heard from him. I could call him, but I don't want to. I want him to call me, but all he ever does is ask Abs about me. If I'm honest, I might actually be even more sad than I look, a wholly unwelcome thought.

"What's got you down," Claire asks stirring whatever fancy coffee she has. Claire and I have been saying hello in the halls ever since we met at the party at Tommy's, and we started meeting out here to chat. We like a lot of the same things, but she also kind of reminds me of Jordan in some ways and right now that is really comforting. Luckily, it's turned out to be a lot of fun learning about her and Devin and their plans for the future so I don't feel so bad about originally thinking of her as a "temporary Jordan's personality replacement" since now I really like being her friend and look forward to these chats. "Troubles with the family, an ex, friends?"

"An ex, I guess," I say thinking that I still don't know if I consider Jordan and I finished yet, and then I think that after six months of silence I must be pretty pathetic to still hold out hope. Is this what love is always like, I wonder, and hope the answer is no.

"Do you want to talk about it?"

"Nope, I've talked it to death at this point, but it still hurts."

"I get that." She stirs her drink again, and looks off in the distance for a minute. "Would you like a distraction?"

However unlikely, a distraction seems like a wonderful idea, so I say, "Give it a shot."

She stirs her drink, bites her lip, and looks off into space. I hadn't noticed it before, but this is the first time since the night of the party that I've seen her look nervous. We have chatted in the halls of school and here in this bookstore when she is studying and I am journaling a few dozen times since that night, but today she seems nervous again, and I don't know why. I wonder what is going on.

"Okay," she says, "I'm trusting you a lot here, but I need to ask you for a favor," she looks around for a minute, "A favor that needs to be kind of private."

I admit it. I was intrigued. "Okay, what's up?"

"Well, you remember Charlotte from the party that night?" Did I remember Charlotte? I start chuckling, and she says, "Of course you do, okay, so, Charlotte has had a crush on someone for a very long time, and she asked me to find out if it was possible for her to get with this person." She starts biting her inner lip again, but suddenly I don't think I like where this conversation is going.

"Um, look, let me just say that if this is about me I'm in no condition to be dating, um, not that Charlotte doesn't seem great, but I'm a little…" While I'm speaking, Claire finally relaxes, and starts laughing pretty loud. She is holding her chest and giggling quite a bit by the time I stop talking. Okay, I am intrigued again. "What?"

"Charlotte has no interest in you so put that out of your head. You would be much more my type. This is not about you."

I feel relieved immediately. Okay, this is not about me, which is good. I don't know what she means about types at the moment, but I will learn that soon enough. Okay, wait, if it's not about me, then why was she so nervous, I wonder. And then, I ask, "Well, then why do you seem so nervous about this?"

"Can I trust you to keep this private?"

I think I know what's going on now. Charlotte likes another girl. That's got to be it because right now Claire reminds me of Jordan and me and others I've met like us. Charlotte has a crush on a girl that I know, and they want me to talk to the girl. Well, that would mean, "She likes Abs doesn't she," I ask with a smile.

Looking around to see if anyone is listening, which I myself have done so many times, Claire whispers, "Yes, she likes Abs and has since they were at that arts camp." I didn't know Charlotte went to the arts camp. Charlotte is not the girl Abs described from the camp based on appearance, but otherwise I have no way of knowing who Abs might like or find attractive. "That night," Claire says, "The night we met," I nod, "Charlotte was going to tell Abs how she felt, but when she went to talk to her, Abs was kissing some guy, and Charlotte got so upset she got wasted, and ended up a mess upstairs."

"Which is when I met her?"

"Yep."

Although it was no big deal at the time, Abs met a new guy named Trevor that night that was a good kisser. They had been trying to date since then, but it wasn't working out and Abs was already bored with him because, as she said, "I'm figuring out I can't fix stupid." I doubted there was any way that Claire or Charlotte knew any of this, and I was sure they didn't know that Abs found a woman attractive at the arts camp. I sat there quietly for a little while thinking about how to broach the subject with Abs.

Claire misinterpreted my lack of speech, and said, "You're not upset now are you?"

"Huh," I asked genuinely confused.

"That Charlotte likes girls, you're not one of those people?" Laughing because it was just too damn funny that this conversation started as I was sitting around pining over my ex boyfriend, I said, "Oh, no, I think its great that Charlotte knows what she wants, and is willing to go for it. I was just thinking about Abs, and how I might bring this up with her since that's what I assume you're asking me to do, you know, the favor."

Relaxing fully for the first time since the conversation started and finally taking a sip of her drink, Claire says, "Oh good, I was pretty sure you were okay to talk to, but you never know, you know."

Oh boy did I know, but I said, "Yep."

"So, what do you think," she asks.

"I think that with Charlotte's permission, I should talk to Abs. I honestly do not know if she would be interested or not, and I would rather not try to guess. That said, I would want to hear its okay from Charlotte so I don't accidentally share a secret she doesn't want shared. I'm sorry if that seems odd to you, but it matters to me."

"Nope, I would do the same thing. If you give me your number, I'll tell Charlotte to call you when she is ready."

"That works for me."

Stirring her drink again, Claire says, "It is so nerve racking, you know? I can only imagine what it is like for Charlotte feeling so nervous all the time about telling anyone anything. I don't know how she does it or other people for that matter."

"I'm sure it takes a lot of energy, patience, and strength."

"I bet," she says, "Can we talk about something easier?"

"Sure," I say, "How is Devin doing and how are the plans for the fall going?" Devin is a sophomore at the University of South Carolina where she will start taking classes in the fall. They have been working out the plans for living together once she gets to Columbia since she got her acceptance letter and danced around the school library with it. I watch her shoulders relax as she tells me about this cute bungalow for rent they found over the weekend.

CHAPTER 34

After Claire left the bookstore, I stayed around writing in my journal for about another hour. It was just another Thursday for the bookstore staff, but for me it marked 17 years on the planet. I write stories about the number 17, and think about where I might be in 17 more years. For whatever reason, I always find myself imagining a future in Atlanta. Ever since I encountered the city the year before, I just somehow see myself there every time I try to picture the future. I like this image, and with it in my head, I head out of the bookstore.

I've just exited the doorway, and turned to the right when I see him. Standing there smoking a cigarette of his own, he looks like a dream, and for a minute, I'm pretty sure I am imagining him. I blink once, twice, really hard a third time, but he is still there. He is looking at me. I am looking at him. Happy birthday I guess.

"Hey," Jordan says flicking ashes from his cigarette.

I light my own, and respond, "Hi."

I start to turn away, and he says, "Are we ever going to talk to each other again?" I pause, just for a moment. He seizes that moment and continues, "I know I screwed up bad, and I'm sorry, so sorry. I miss you so much, and if there is anything I can do tell me and I'll do it, anything. Yell at me if you want to, just talk to me please."

"If you wanted to talk to me, if you miss me so much, why haven't I heard from you in so long Jordan?" My voice sounds cold even to my own ears. I can feel all the anger, all the sadness, all of it just bubbling up inside me. But I can also feel love, longing, and how much I miss him. I don't know which set of feelings is stronger, but both feel too strong for me at the moment.

"I," he gulps, I think he's scared, "I, uh, I thought you didn't want to talk to me. The way you left the house, I thought it was over and I didn't want to make it worse by pressuring you. I should have called, I guess, I don't know." So once again he tried to guess what I felt and got it completely wrong! I feel rage pumping through me. I hate his assumptions. I hate this moment. I hate everything, all of it!

"Are you ever going to learn that trying to guess what I feel doesn't work," that was anger talking, it was boiling over, why did he always guess instead of talking to me about things, "Huh Jordan, are you ever gonna learn that you're really fucking terrible at guessing games?" I'm shaking, and I don't feel like I'm in control of my body or the words I'm saying. "Are you going to ever stop guessing and just talk to me, instead of jumping to conclusions?"

Jordan's whole body appears to shrink right in front of me. He stares at his shoes, stutters a bit, and finally says, "I want to." His voice sounds so weak, and to my horror, he reminds me of Roger that day in the parking lot, beaten, defeated, and scared. His whole body is slumping like he is waiting to be hit by something. Where is his confidence? His charm? He looks like he has no clue what he is doing. "Do you think, if I, uh, you know, can talk about things, do you think you could ever forgive me," he says in that same broken voice. He looks like I've felt the past six months, and part of me really wants to hug him, forgive him, and start over. But I'm not ready for that yet, and I don't know if I ever will be. It all still hurts so damn much, and I don't want to feel this way again next year.

I wipe my face, exhale deeply, and say, "I really don't know Jordan. I really don't know." His body somehow appears to shrink even more, and I move toward him and raise his head the way I used to so I can see his eyes. Softly, I say, "I don't know, but I really want to." I can see the tears in his eyes, and the pain there too. It matches my own. For the first time in what seems like forever, we're only inches apart from each other physically, but I don't know if we can close the emotional gap or not.

"What can I do," he asks, his voice breaking again.

"Well," I say, my voice going a little bit cold again, "You can start by letting me hear from you from time to time, and we can see where things go from there. You can try to talk to me for a change, and maybe give up the guessing shit. That would be a good start I think, but, you know, it's up to you, mate."

With these words, I feel him start to cry again, and I begin walking away. I feel his eyes on me as I move into the parking lot, and I turn around twice and see him just watching me leave. I don't know why he just stands there, and part of me wants to run back up to him and somehow just fix all this right away. But I know that won't work. I'm still too angry, too sad. When I make it to my car, there is an envelope on the windshield. I pick it up, open it, and remove a card that has crudely drawn candles all over the front of a pale yellow background, and a little crudely drawn chicken saying, "Not enough candles in the world…" and inside, the card says, "To light up the sky like you do," and below that, it says, in Jordan's handwriting, "Happy Birthday, I love you, I'm sorry, Jordan."

I hold the first example of written evidence of us in my hands, and look up at the front of the building. Somehow, even in that moment, I know I will keep this little piece of flimsy cardboard for a long time. I still can't go back yet, but I really want to. I look at the building. Jordan is still standing there. I wave. He waves. I get in my car, wipe the tears from my face, and drive out of the parking lot. As I leave the store, I can see Jordan still standing there in my rearview mirror and I watch until he fades out of sight. On the way home, I stop at the rest area right past the South Carolina border, pull out the card, and read it again. I sit there reading it over and over again with tears rolling down my face as I try to figure out whether or not I'll be able to move past the last six months.

CHAPTER 35

"I talked to Jordan yesterday," I say as Abs comes bouncing down the ledge to our little spot by the river. We haven't been here in a while so we decided that we should come back for a little chat. The water is calming as usual, but I'm more interested in the fact that my parents told me Jordan called this morning. I didn't call him back. I wanted to meet up with Abs. But I hope he calls again.

"Wow, what was that like?"

"Hard."

"So, are you two done or are you gonna try to fix it?"

"I still don't know. He said he stayed away because he thought I wanted him to, but he apologized and seemed like he really wanted to fix things. I don't know, but I guess we will see."

"That makes sense. Do you want it to work out?"

"Yes, I still love him and I want what we had back, but I just don't know if we can get back there after all that's happened. I want us to, I knew that more last night than I have before, but I just don't know if I can. I don't know if we can."

Abs lights a smoke for her, another for me, and says, "What else is new?"

"Well, now that you ask, I know someone who happens to have a crush on you."

"Really? Are they at least interesting?"

"Well, I don't know if they could possibly be as smart as Trevor my dear."

"Shut up, don't make me remind you about the storeroom."

"Okay, okay, how is ole Trevor?"

"Done, over. I don't know what I was thinking."

"I don't think you were thinking, I think you were fantasizing about that chest."

"His chest is so pretty."

"Don't I know it?"

"So who is in love with me this time?"

About a half hour after I got home the night before, the phone rang and my mom said it was someone named Charlotte. I took the cordless phone out on the back porch after making sure my mom hung up, and talked to Charlotte for about an hour. The first part of the conversation involved her thanking me for how I acted at the party. I accepted her thanks, but at the same time, I kept thinking that it says something terrible about our world when someone feels the need to be thankful that another person did not hurt and violate them. The second part of the conversation involved Abs. Charlotte admitted that she was scared, and that very few people knew that she liked girls, but she thought it was best to find out because she was losing her mind over "what if" questions. I checked a few times to make sure, but ultimately, she made it very clear that she wanted me to tell Abs how she felt. I told her I didn't know when I would bring it up with Abs, but I promised I would do it and keep it quiet.

"First you need to promise me that you will keep this one quiet. Lock it in the vault, especially if you're not into it – got it?"

"Ooh, this sounds interesting. Yes, of course, you have my word. If I'm interested I will be discreet, and if I'm not interested no one will ever know that I know unless it's okay. Does that work?" Honestly, I had no worries about Abs outing anyone, but at the same time, I promised Charlotte I would take all possible precautions. The fact was that if Abs had any interest in juicy, dangerous secrets she could easily destroy me, Jordan and probably a few dozen other people any day of the week. That was, conservatively speaking, about the least likely thing in the world.

"Yes, that works," I said giggling, "So, do you remember a girl named Charlotte that was at the arts camp with you?"

"The little blonde girl that looked like a real life tinker bell?" To my utter shame, I had not thought of this description, but it was dead on the head. Charlotte really did look so much like the tinker bell cartoon from our childhood.

"Yeah, I think that's the one. She goes to our school, she's a senior and hangs out with Claire."

"Oh my god, she is so cute!"

"True."

"She has a crush on me?"

"Yes, she does, and apparently she has for quite a while now, but it really hit her at the camp, and she's been trying to work up the courage to talk to you, but ultimately, I was drafted for the job."

"Why?"

"She actually wanted to tell you at Tommy's party, but you were busy with Trevor."

"Ooh, that probably wasn't fun for her."

"Nope, probably like a conversation with him for you," I said and we both started laughing.

"Does she know I like girls, or I might like girls?"

"No, I didn't tell her or Claire anything about you. I wouldn't do that without your permission, you know that."

"That's what I thought, but I wanted to be sure."

"What do you think?"

Abs just sits there for a few minutes twirling her hair. She lights another cigarette, and stares out at the woods. She smiles at me, looks at her hair, smiles again, and takes a puff off of her cigarette. "I think I'm interested, but I'm not sure, this is, you know, new for me. She's really cute, but I don't know if I can be, you know, be with, you know, a girl." She pulls on a piece of her hair, adopts a rather whiney voice, and says, "What should I do mom?"

Laughing and shoving her just a little bit, I say, "Well, my child, if you're interested you should talk to her, and if that is fun, maybe hang out with her, and if that is fun, maybe see if something happens. If it does, good for you. If it doesn't, good for you again. That's the best advice I got. At the very least, she'll probably be more interesting than Trevor."

"Oh shut up, radio static is more interesting than Trevor."

"Well, I have her number if you want it."

"I want it. I don't know if I'll use it yet, but I want it."

"Sounds good to me. I won't tell her we talked about it yet so you can take your time and make up your own mind whether or not you want to call."

Twirling her hair, she says, "Yeah," and smiles, "Do that."

CHAPTER 36

After our chat, Abs stayed at the river to do some writing, and I headed back toward my house. I walked up the dirt path that had been there as long as I could remember, and found myself enjoying the smells and sounds of the woods. It was a little strange to realize how rarely I walked in these woods nowadays after spending most of my life doing so almost daily. I looked out over the ravine, and the big black pipe we used to crawl across to get to the other side of it when we were kids. It didn't look so big anymore, and I wonder if there was a time when this town felt big that I just could not recall.

As I reached the walkway that used to be an abandoned railroad track, I turned left in the direction of home. The park was behind me, and the walkway stretched out as far as I could see, winding its way through what still felt like "my" woods. The path Jordan and I made and hid from plain sight was also behind me, about halfway back to the park, and for a moment I thought about going there. Instead, I kept walking toward my side of the neighborhood via the walkway that once caked my shoes with mud on rainy days, but now felt colder with it's new concrete surface.

As I walked, I heard movement in the woods to my right, between the track and the backyards of various homes, and turned to see Zach bouncing out of the woods. "What are you up to," I said, and must have startled him because he almost jumped out of his skin.

"What's up man, how you doing?"

"I'm good. I was hanging out with Abs down on the river. Been a while buddy, how you been doing," I said as he came closer, and I reached out to smack him on the back. Before my hand could land, however, he moved quickly, wincing a little bit, to avoid my hand. I was a little surprised since he was the originator of the whole pat on the back ritual. I remembered him trying to convince me that it would look wrong if boys were hugging hello and goodbye.

"You know, it's been, you know, it's cool," He said rubbing his stomach and looking around like he was scared of something or looking for something or maybe both.

"Hey, you okay man?"

"Yeah, no, Yeah, I'm cool, I just had a fall the other day out here so I'm, you know, watching where I go and you know, still a little sore man." He kept fidgeting and looking around as he spoke, but he said he was okay so I figured he knew best.

"You wanna come back to my place man, my dad's got some of those pills he takes for his back, might be good for the soreness."

"Nah man, it's cool. I got some stuff, and I'm actually supposed to be meeting up with Jordan, you know, so I should get back over to the park and get my car." He looks around in all directions again. Man, he always seems so strange to me, but I feel like this is even more than usual. I wonder what him and Jordan are up to, but I don't want to ask. I don't want to risk sounding the way I feel when I think of Jordan. After a minute of silence and looking around all over the place, he says, "But you know, thanks man, I appreciate it," and he turns and starts heading toward the park. When he came out of the woods, it looked like we were going in the same direction, but I guess not since his car is back at the park.

I watch him stroll down the walkway, he is kind of swerving a little bit instead of walking in a straight line, and I try to remember if he always does that, but I don't see him enough these days to really have any clue. I don't know what it is, but something seems off or maybe just different about him. For a moment, a question floats across my mind. If he is so sore and supposed to be meeting Jordan, what was he doing roaming around in the woods? It doesn't make any sense, but then again, Zach never makes a lot of sense to me. Hell, I think, from what Jordan and Abs have said, I often make just as little sense to him come to think about it.

I stand there watching him move down the path for a few more seconds until I hear sounds behind me, and quickly turn around to see what is there. It's just a family out for a stroll on the new walkway. I laugh at myself a little bit. After so many years of having this place to ourselves and keeping an eye out for anything from bullies to snakes to adults while we were up to no good, it still sometimes startles me that people just come out here now for recreation. Giggling, I imagine the day where the river swing is a complete recreational swimming area with less beer cans left behind, and a lifeguard on duty. Maybe they'll build a playground in the little patch by the stream where Jordan and I used to sit around and daydream as kids. Maybe one day there won't be any woods at all.

I'm surprised to realize that this thought is both happy and sad for me. I'm sad at the loss of what this area used to be, and the freedom and privacy it held for us as kids. I wonder where future kids will go to get away from their parents, teachers, and churches. Where will they learn to make out, try drugs and alcohol, and have imaginary adventures? On the other hand, I kind of like the idea of "my" woods not being around when I am gone. So much of my early life took place here, and so many memories are buried in the ground, hidden by the underbrush, sheltered by the ravines. I kind of like that no one will be able to get to them, that they may be the last of their kind. Wherever future kids grow up, these woods will likely only remain the way they were for me in my own memory.

I'm still thinking about these things as I reach the street with the parking lot for the public pool. The pool is another thing that seems so strange when I see it now. Once upon a time, it was full of families every summer, and never ending baseball games out on the front lawn. It was messy and crowded and ours. We swam and dared each other to go on the high slide and ended up in fights over meaningless baseball games. It was another part of the whole growing up thing, like the woods, like the park.

After it closed for the season this past year, new owners took over, and the evidence of their presence was visible as we came closer to the new season. The fences had been renovated, and it was harder to see inside the place. The paint had been replaced, and a more formal baseball field had been put in down the hill from the pool and away from the now manicured front lawn. My parents told me this year the pool would be charging membership fees to everyone instead of only for families who lived beyond the borders of the neighborhood, and Abs' parents heard that there was a new set of rules for "appropriate conduct and dress" going into effect as well.

As I passed the parking lot where Claire parked her car that night in December, it hit me that even in our sleepy little town it seemed like everything was changing as the millennium drew to a close. In many cases, I felt the same way I felt about the woods – happy and sad at the same time. I thought about my ongoing plans to leave the area after high school, and I wondered if I would recognize the place at all if I came back to visit some time in the future.

CHAPTER 37

When I got home that evening, Jordan had called again. This time, I called him back, and we spent about an hour talking about school, his church, and my adventures with Abs. At the time, I didn't think to wonder why he wasn't hanging out with Zach after I had just been told they were supposed to meet up in the evening. I was so focused on the phone call that I didn't really think about anything else at the time, but later, I wondered if Zach made that up for some reason and what that reason could have been. On the phone, Jordan was looking forward to a camping trip with the basketball team later in the spring. I told him about my journaling habits, and that I was starting to consider college. It was a little tense, but it was also nice to be talking to each other again. At the end of the call, he told me he loved me. I hesitated, but then I told him I loved him too.

Over the next few months, Jordan and I spoke regularly over the phone, and even met at the park a few times. It wasn't the same as when we were younger, but nothing seemed to be the same anymore. It seemed like high school changed so much without any of us noticing it was happening. I remember standing in our spot one afternoon, and realizing that I couldn't remember the last time I had been there with or without Jordan. When we were younger, before the cars and trips across the river, before the walking path and the renovations to the pool, we came to the park separately or together almost every day. I thought about Abs and I making plans to go sit out on the river, and how absurd that would have seemed when we practically lived in the woods behind her house as kids.

I remember one day Jordan and I were walking in the woods, and he started talking about Zach's new girlfriend. She was a softball player at one of the private schools in Augusta, and she intimidated almost everyone she met without really trying to. None of these details caught my attention because in that moment I realized I almost never saw Zach anymore. The only time I had really seen him in the past year had been the day in the woods when he seemed nervous and scared. We lived and slept just a few blocks from each other. Other than Abs, he was physically closer to where I lived than anyone I knew, but I almost never saw or heard from him at all. The day in the woods was it, and that was purely by accident and only for a few minutes. I didn't go to the bus stop over by his house anymore because I drove to school. I didn't hang out on the basketball court in front of his school anymore because I went to the one near the bookstore so I could write after working out. We still lived just as close to each other, but we existed in different worlds.

The expansion of worlds seemed to be a theme running through that spring and summer as our junior year came to a close and Jordan and I sought to reconnect. Through a program at his church, Jordan was looking at funds that might allow him to attend college. I was staring at maps and college brochures for places in Atlanta. Abs was researching a liberal arts school on the border of North and South Carolina. Zach was, according to Jordan, putting in his initial paperwork for joining the military, and hoping he would get to travel the world soon. Jordan and I were sitting by the river holding hands for the first time in almost a year in late May when he told me he was going out west over the summer with a group from his church. "We're going to learn about fellowship, and missionary work with other churches. I'll be gone most of July and August."

We had been back in contact for three months, and I remember rubbing his finger a little bit as I said, "That sounds like a good opportunity for you. Are you excited?"

"I am, but I'm also worried about us. We're finally starting to spend time together again. I don't want to go on this trip if it will cause problems for us."

"Why would it cause problems for us?"

"Well," he paused and threw out his cigarette, "Lenny will be on the trip, so will some of the others who don't like you because of, you know, how you are, and I don't want to mess up again. I don't want to ruin the chance of us being us again by doing something stupid or because you start worrying about me out west with them."

Smiling and honestly impressed with how open Jordan is becoming about his fears and worries, I say, "You have to let the opinions of other people go babe. Think about how many people don't like you because of how you are, they're wrong and so are the people who can't understand how I am. It's that simple. The breeders don't understand you, and the fundamentalist gays, as Abs calls them, don't understand me – that doesn't matter. What matters is you and I understand each other, talk to each other, and try not to fall for the bigotry of other people. This trip is something you would love so I think you should do it."

Jordan nods his head, and smiles, "And what about us?"

"Honestly, I think the trip might be good for us too, not just for you. We've had fun the last few months, but I'm still hesitant and you're still scared. Maybe those couple months give us time to trust each other, fool around with people if we want to, and come back in the fall and see how we feel. Maybe a little break after these months together is exactly what we need to start over."

"So, like now, we kind of stay friends, and take our time?"

"Yeah, I think it might be good. We know we love each other, and we have a whole life ahead of us, right? Let's just keep taking things slow, and see what it looks like after the summer when we've had more time away from last September."

With that, Jordan and I had a plan for the summer. He would go on his trip, and we would think about what we wanted to be going forward. I think we both knew that whatever happened, the past year taught us a lot. We both knew we loved each other since we were eight and eight-and-a-half-years-old respectively, but we learned just how much we could hurt each other and just how easy it would be to lose what we had. Those were important lessons going forward, as they often are for so many young lovers. We sat there by the river, that day and other days before he left in July, beginning to touch again, beginning to kiss again, beginning to figure out what we wanted the future to look like, and most importantly, beginning to learn how to make the future we wanted more likely.

We weren't the only ones figuring things out as that spring turned to summer. In another part of town a few weeks later, Abs sat on the back porch at her house kissing Charlotte for the first time. They spent the end of the school year passing notes, talking on the phone, and talking at school. Abs was certain that Charlotte was one of the most interesting people she had ever known, but she was still unsure about being with another girl. She showed up at my house in early June, and told me, "I think I really like her."

"That's good right?"

"I don't know."

"Why not," I asked lighting a smoke.

"I know I like talking to her. I like hanging out with her, you know. I like her, but I don't know about, you know, the other stuff."

"Ah, you're not sure if you "like, like" her?"

"How can I find out for sure?"

Laughing, I say, "I'm not sure you can find out for sure in some grand way, but you can find out with Charlotte by just giving it a shot. I mean, in my case, I thought boys were cute and I liked hanging out with them, some of them, when I was little, but I didn't really know I liked boys – or girls either honestly – until Jordan kissed me one day after soccer and then Lena and I kissed later that year when I was, remember, being "So silly she couldn't stand it." When Jordan kissed me, I liked it. I liked it a lot. It kind of scared me how much I liked it. I felt the same way with Lena. I liked it, and that's how I knew – same thing with Jessica, same thing with what's his name. I tried it, and I liked it, simple as that."

"You know, she still calls you silly sometimes?"

"Honey, she still calls me silly all the damn time," I say and we both laugh at this little nickname.

"So, about Charlotte, I should try it?"

"Only if you want to Abs. But yeah, if you like her, but don't know if its more than a friend thing, the only way I know to find out is to try it. There might be other ways, but that's the only one I know. In the end, though, it's your call. I don't think anyone can tell you whether or not you should try it with Charlotte or anyone."

"But that will tell me how I feel?"

"Kind of, I mean, it will tell you how you feel about Charlotte. I kissed other boys and other girls that I didn't end up liking. I mean, I thought they were cute, but kissing them was like nothing, I didn't like it, I didn't like them. So, you could kiss Charlotte and like it, but that doesn't mean now you like all girls, or you could kiss Charlotte and not like it, but that doesn't mean you don't like girls at all. I think its more complicated than what you can get from one person, I think, for me, I always have to try and see."

"I get that, I mean, I thought I would like Trevor, but just no. I thought I hated Zach, but loved kissing him. It was completely different, but they were both boys."

"So did the last time ever actually happen?"

"Yes, of course, Zach and I slept together again a couple weeks ago, his softball star doesn't know and neither does Charlotte, but its okay because that was definitely the last time, I mean, this time there is no doubt."

"I do not believe you at all just so you know."

"Me neither," she says and we both start laughing. "I don't know what it is about him, but it always seems to come back?"

"I've been in love with the same two people pretty much all my life, yep, I know."

"True, you really have no room to talk, but what about this time, you know, with Charlotte, I mean, it should be like that right?"

"Yeah, I mean, I think so Abs. I think it's the same whether the people are boys, girls, or something else. I don't think that stuff really matters, but that might just be for me because there are people like Jordan and Greg who only like boys and then Zach seems to only like girls, so maybe its different for them. Taylor always said she only really found herself attracted to people like Nick or people like me. So, I think it really depends and you kind of just have to figure out how it works for you and what you feel drawn to if that makes sense. This or that type of body or person might not fit for a lot of people, but for me, best I can tell, you only know if you like them enough by trying it out and seeing how you feel." I remember wishing I had better answers for Abs, hell for all of us, but even now I'm not sure there is one good answer. The same way that other people seem to have always felt drawn to one type of person or body, I've always felt drawn to many different people, and not really cared about the body type all that much. I wondered just how many variations there were in the ways people felt about these things.

"You ever wish there was an easier way?"

"I've been moping around most of the year over the love of my life who cheated on me, what do you think?"

Abs just starts laughing. We sit together for a while talking about how complicated our lives have become, and reminiscing about the days where all we seemed to worry about was the latest record by Madonna or Janet Jackson. We watch the sun, and just enjoy the cozy simplicity one only seems to find in friendships that last for a long time. With all the changes that have taken place, there is something comforting in the things that stay the same.

I look down at her ever-present Winnie the Pooh purse that somehow became a sex symbol to some of the guys at school. It looks battered, worn on the edges, and it now relies on safety pins for some of its structural integrity. The colors are faded, and I remember when they looked brand new. The thing has been all over this town, visited the hot spots in Augusta, danced to the poetry and music of an arts camp, and will likely soon make its debut on a college campus.

On the outside, stains, dirt, and faded colors tell a kind of story. Together, they probably look a lot like we do on the inside after all these years. On the inside, though, there is still a sanctuary for all that remains important to Abs. I just stare at the bag. It reminds me of simpler times and enduring dreams. I run my hands through Abs' hair as she puts her head on my shoulder, and I wonder, are we ready for whatever the next adventure is?

CHAPTER 38

"Now that takes me back," Lena says with her head on my chest in the middle of the afternoon on the day I arrive in Atlanta that August. I light a cigarette, take a puff, and pass it to her. She drags on the cigarette as I run my hands down the length of her bare back accidentally tickling her in the process. Her body has changed in the years since we last found ourselves tangled up in this way. It is stronger and softer at the same time. Her hips have filled out a little bit so she's a little bigger than her teenage self, and her arms have gained a tension and power from pounding on an electric guitar.

She passes the cigarette back to me after a couple of puffs, and softly kisses me on the chest before sighing deeply and resting her head right between my nipples. We haven't been this way, post orgasm linked by sweat, in quite a while, but it still feels safe and beautiful like it did when we were younger. As I take a puff off the cigarette using one hand, my other hand rubs the small of her back, and traces the same three random freckles that fascinated me years ago. We have nowhere to be and nowhere to go, so we just lay there soaking in the moment, and ignoring the rest of the world.

I don't know if I would call what happened this afternoon a planned activity, but it was on my mind as I drove to Atlanta to visit Lena again. Last year, before Nick headed south for Florida and Taylor's new job at an amusement park, I spent a wonderful weekend here with Lena, Nick, and Taylor that ended in a horrible fashion when I got home. I thought about this series of events a few nights earlier when Jordan called. I told him I was going to Atlanta for the week, and he asked – instead of accusing me – if I still had feelings for Lena. I told him that I did, and that I might always.

This time, however, his reaction was different. "I think you should explore how you feel about her," he said. "I think you need to know what the two of you have, and how it effects you and me. And I think I need that too going forward." I agreed, and he told me to have fun and we started talking about all the fun he was having out in Arizona, and a guy named Bill he found himself hanging out with a lot. I told him he, "Should see if there is something there. It might be good for you to open yourself up to possibilities, and I'll be here for you no matter what as long as you're honest with me." He said he'd think about it, and we said goodnight.

The next day I was on the phone with Lena finalizing plans for the trip, getting directions to her newest apartment, and I told her about the conversation I had with Jordan. At first, she got really quiet on the phone, and I wondered if I had said something foolish or wrong. Then, after a few seconds and what sounded like her lighting a cigarette, she said, "I think you know that I love you, and I think you know that in some way I always have, I mean, you're the only one from that town I still talk to other than Abs, and her and I mainly talk about you and whoever she's dating these days." I listened to her words and thought about just how rarely you heard about people moving away and continuing to talk to the same people from their old town regularly for years. "The thing is silly, you know you love me, and I could probably share you with Jordan and be fine as long as I was allowed to go out and flirt and date too. And I think you would like that honestly, but I don't know if Jordan could do that."

I was drawn back to fantasies earlier in life of having more than one significant other, and to my back and forth internal debate about Jessica versus Jordan. "And, if I'm honest, I don't think you'll ever be fully happy without Jordan so most likely y'all will be a couple and we will be us, like we always have, and I'm okay with that because that is one option that always seems like it could let all three of us be happy in our own ways." I didn't know what to say. This was the same girl who kept surprising me over and over again throughout my life, and here she had done it again. In a nutshell, in a very simple way, she had basically spoken things I'd felt for years, but never been able to put into words. I didn't know what to say.

After what seemed like too much silence, I said, "I think you're probably right." We talked for a few more minutes about the trip, and how much we were looking forward to hanging out. I will always be amazed by just how fast a conversation could go from casual, no big deal, goofy to serious and back again with Lena. She had this ability to cut through all the bullshit in a way that I still envy to this day. When we got off the phone, I packed my bags, wrote in my journal for a while, and went to sleep.

Lena rubbed her head against my chest, and said, "I want coffee," in a tired voice. I ran my hands through her hair, slid her off of me, and went into the kitchen. I started the coffeemaker, and looked at the picture she kept of us from the night at the bar on the side of her kitchen counter. There we stood, Lena and I in flowing skirts beside Taylor and Nick in perfect pressed pantsuits, ready for an adventure in East Point. I went back to the bedroom, and she kicked at me with her foot in a goofy gesture. I brought her some coffee, and we spent the afternoon in bed talking and kicking the air.

That night on the phone, I would tell Jordan her kicking reminded me of the spasms you see little animals make when their sleep is disturbed unexpectedly. That night on the phone, I would learn that Jordan also had sex that day. That night on the phone, I would realize that Lena was right, that I could share them if we were all honest with each other, and we were all free to follow our desires. That night on the phone, Jordan would let me know that he really just wanted it to be the two of us if that was possible. That night, as I hung up the phone, I started trying to figure out what I wanted.

Lena and I spent the week roaming around Atlanta. Even though Nick no longer lived there, we went out to East Point to visit that old house. Even though the club we went to the summer before had shut down, we wore matching skirts out to dinner one night, and took them off each other – something we both thought about but didn't do the year before – when we got back to her place. Even though Jordan was many states away, I thought I saw him everywhere. Even though I was in love with Lena, I started to think she might be right about my inability to give up Jordan even if that meant embracing monogamy.

On my last night in town, Lena asked me to go with her to a meeting at her college. She went to the public university downtown. She wanted to go into marketing if she couldn't turn music into a career, and use the marketing knowledge she had for her art if she could turn music into a career. The university kind of blended into the downtown skyline. Aside from little logos here and there, it was hard to tell we were actually on a college campus. It was the end of the summer, so there wasn't a lot of activity in the buildings, but there was still something about the place that spoke to me. The old walls, the bulletin boards with faculty and student accomplishments, the smell of fresh cleaning products mingling with old books – there was something special about this place.

At first, Lena was hesitant about the meeting. She turned to me in bed that morning, and said, "I really want to go to this meeting at school tonight, and I want you to come with me, but…" She fell silent, and I asked but what. She looked down at the bed, and said, "Well it's about relationships with multiple partners and other alternative families and groups, and I don't want it to seem like I'm trying to push you in that direction, but I'm really interested in the topic. But I want to spend the night with you, so we don't have to go to this thing if it would make you uncomfortable."

I thought the idea sounded fascinating, and I told her so. We went to the meeting, and listened to people talk about what it was like to love multiple people, raise families with multiple parents, and navigate relationships where people had different sexual interests. In some cases, the relationships contained three or four people who were all in love with and attracted to each other. In other cases, it was just two people who each gave the other the freedom to go out and date on their own whenever they wanted to. In still other cases, there were groups of three people where one of them was bisexual and the other two were heterosexual and gay and the three had a relationship together, but also were allowed to go out with other people. I was amazed at what seemed like endless possibilities.

I remembered as a kid that almost no one in the Bible seemed to only marry one person, but when I asked about this it made people angry. I wondered why they didn't just tell us about these other options. I wondered how many people were doing this. I wondered if it was something like being gay or bisexual or trans, where it was really common, but people just did not talk about it or know about it. I wondered what it would be like, maybe like this weekend where I was on the phone with Jordan at least once a day and hanging out with Lena at the same time, to actually be in one of these types of relationships. I thought about this possibility all the way back to Lena's place, and we sat up most of the night talking about it and looking over the materials the people at the meeting gave us.

Lena became interested in the topic in her first semester at the university when she took a class taught by a woman who was in a poly – another new term for me at the time – relationship. Lena noticed that she often fell hard for transmen and female people, but she was mostly sexually attracted to certain types of male bodies. She wondered how she might have intimate relationships with people who did not fit the body type she wanted to have sex with, and thought maybe she could try what the teacher did in a different way. She also found herself attracted to – usually without knowing it ahead of time – bisexual males, but worried about having a relationship with someone who wanted things she did not have. Over the past year, she learned everything she could about the possibilities, and the more she learned, the more she wanted to know.

This never-ending curiosity was something we always had in common. That night, she let me borrow some of the books she had been reading, and I put them in my bags planning to spend the fall catching up on the subject. Hours later, we fell into bed and into each other one last time before I headed back to South Carolina. Later, as we laid in bed in the early morning hours, she said, "I want you to know that whatever happens I'll always be here silly. You'll figure out what is best for you, and for you and Jordan, just give yourself the space and time and it'll all make sense at some point." Those words, though simple and not unexpected from her, rattled around my head all the way back home.

CHAPTER 39

When I returned from Atlanta, senior year was waiting on me. Seventeen years old with pretty good grades, damn good friends, and a lot of confusion about once again feeling like I was in love with two people at the same time in different ways, I walked the hallways at school already saying goodbye to the town I had always wanted to leave. A couple weeks into the school year, I went by my locker at the end of the day, and found a note from Abs telling me to come by the house that night. We had not hung out since I got back from Atlanta, and I automatically felt giddy about the opportunity.

When I arrived at her house that evening, Abs poured us both glasses of wine, and we sat on the back porch. After taking a sip of her wine, Abs looked at me and said, "I went for it."

"Really?"

"Yep, I was thinking about you trying to figure out all the Jordan stuff, going to see Lena, and studying all this new stuff on relationships, and I thought, you know what, I want to know, you know, I just want to know. So, Labor Day weekend I went for it."

"How was it?"

"It was strange, but also good, but also different. Charlotte came over here, and I just told her everything I was feeling about things, and she was really cool about it. She said she understood exactly what I was going through because at the arts camp, the one we went to, there was another girl, a straight girl Charlotte is pretty sure, who developed a crush on her, and had a lot of the same internal debate and stuff, you know, that I was having right now. That girl, your old friend Becca by the way, she was…"

"Wait, wait, what? Becca, Jessica's Becca, are you sure, Becca, the one who thought what's his name had a disease?"

"Yeah, I thought you would get a kick out of that, but yeah."

"Well, huh, I never would have guessed that one."

"Comes in all sizes my friend, isn't that what you told me" she says and we toast our wine glasses. "Kind of makes you want to give her some hell doesn't it?"

"A little bit, but at the same time, I know how hard this shit is, so no."

"Same here," she says sipping her wine for a second afterward. "So, anyway, this girl Becca, you know, she finally gets up the nerve to talk to Charlotte, and they end up making out by the lake at the camp, and it freaks her out like so bad. It's kind of sad. Anyhow, Charlotte figures either Becca didn't like it or liked it more than she wanted to, you know. But the point is, Charlotte was cool about my stuff, you know. She told me, like point blank, she told me she likes me a lot, and she really enjoys hanging out with me so we could try it out if we wanted to, but I needed to promise to tell her everything, you know, like how I felt because she didn't want to get hurt, you know, and I can respect that."

"Charlotte sounds pretty damn cool Abs."

"Oh yeah, she's amazing. She also told me it took her lots of time, like a lot, to figure out that she only wanted to be with girls. She always liked girls, you know, kind of like Jordan has always known he only liked boys, you know, right, but she went through a lot of shit with herself because of other people and all that kind of stuff and wanting to fit in and what not, but after all that, she said she could not tell me just how important it is to really know, you know?"

"I couldn't agree with her more Abs."

"I know, and Jordan told me about the same thing years ago when we were talking about how he feels, you know."

"So, what happened? How do you feel?"

"So, I told her, you know, I promised to be honest, and then I told her, like, whenever she wanted to, she should, you know, make a move. That sounds so silly, but you know what I mean."

Smiling, I say, "Yeah, I know what you mean."

"So, then, like almost right away, you know, she kisses me, and it felt good and it was fun, and we were back here making out for like almost an hour, you know, and I liked it a lot, like, it was a lot of fun and stuff and her body felt good, it was nice."

"I hear a but coming."

"But, you know, it was more like kissing Zach than like kissing Simon, does that make sense?"

"Yep, it was fun and hot, but not mind blowing emotionally."

"Yes, that's it, yes. It was fun, it was hot, like really hot, she is beautiful, but there was like no emotion stuff, no I love you fireworks, you know, nothing like that, just like hot and fun and wow so good, but not like, you know, love, it just felt like playing around, you know, like having fun like it always did with Zach, you know, nothing serious."

"Did you tell her this?"

"Oh yeah, definitely, I mean I told her I would be honest. So, like, after an hour or so or however long it was, we were laying side by side right here, you know, and I told her how I was feeling, you know, that I liked it, I like her, but I didn't really feel anything emotionally. And you know what? She was so fucking cool about it again. She said that it was okay, and that it happens, and of course, I thought about Zach and I told her about that, and it made sense to her, and she told me about this girl that goes to the Prep School over in the city, can't remember the name, but it was a similar thing. She said they fooled around for a long time, but never really dated because it was fun, but nothing else, and that's how I felt."

"Makes a lot of sense Abs, and honestly sounds like what Rachel and Nick experienced way back when. I'm glad you didn't lead her on about it. So, where does that leave the two of you?"

"Well, that's probably the coolest part. We're still hanging out, but more like friends than maybe a couple now, you know, and I told her that I might, you know, want to go farther at some point, you know, I mean, it was a lot of fun being with her like that and maybe sex with her would be a lot of fun too. I mean, that's what happened with Zach over and over again, you know, we had fun and it was hot, you know. But, you know, she said we'll have to wait and see because, and I get this like so clearly you know, but, she has feelings when we hang out and kiss and stuff, and so we shouldn't go further, or even kiss much, if it might lead to her getting hurt. So, we agreed to keep hanging out, and just being honest, you know, and we'll see what happens down the road, it was really cool, she is awesome."

"I think that sounds great Abs."

"Yeah, me too. So, I can be with girls, but like with boys I might or might not actually feel anything for them, its good to know. How are you doing?"

181

"I'm good. Jordan and I went up to the magazine shop today after school, and spent some time hanging out at his house for the first time since last year. It was kind of nice, it didn't feel like before, but it felt good. His skin is just as intoxicating as it ever was, and, I don't know, I feel like we're headed in the right direction."

"What about Lena?"

"I don't know. I've talked to her a couple times since I got back from Atlanta, but Jordan really isn't into the idea of multiple lovers. He says he just doesn't get it, and really wants it to just be the two of us again. I love them both, but its different if that makes sense. Jordan is like my whole life and Lena is too, but with Jordan it's always been like this, but with Lena she was like my friend and role model first, I guess I gotta figure it out. On the bright side, somehow they have both managed to be supportive of me and each other, and I think that, at least, makes this a whole lot easier."

"What are you going to do?"

"I think I'm going to take Lena's advice. I'm going to spend time with Jordan, follow my feelings, and see what happens. I don't really know what to do without Jordan around, and I think she's right that I have to face that, commit to him again if I can, and see where it leads me because if I don't, I'll always wonder what could have been, and I might not be able to really be happy without him. Jordan is open to trying to see if he can wrap his head around the multiple thing, you know, but none of us think he can without giving something up while Lena and I agree we can go in either direction without losing especially now that Jordan is more comfortable with our friendship. So, I think Lena's right, that I need to focus on Jordan and see what that leads to."

"I understand that. Who knows, maybe it will all work out."

"I hope so. Anyhow, he's out with Zach and some of the other guys on the basketball team this weekend, they're having another camping retreat."

"A camping retreat?"

"Yeah, they did it in the spring too. Its supposed to bring them together as a team, but I don't know if it actually does anything more than give a group of guys a chance to sit around and look at porn and talk about chicks."

Laughing, Abs asks, "Is that what they did in the spring?"

"Pretty much, Jordan said most of the weekend was just looking at porn, talking about chicks – their word – while talking about how much cooler they were than other basketball teams."

Abs smacks the deck and laughs so hard she spills some of her wine, "Oh, I bet Jordan just loves that."

"Oh you bet, nothing excites Jordan more than talking about all the chicks he wants to bang," I say and we both roar with laughter at the thought of Jordan, the same guy who has to turn his head when Abs changes clothes, talking about all the women he's going to get. "According to him, its basically a bunch of stupid guys being stupid for the hell of it."

"That's kind of what I imagined when you said basketball camping retreat."

CHAPTER 40

In late October, I got a phone call from Claire. She said she was feeling homesick, and wondered if I might want to come up for a visit. Devin was up in North Carolina participating in a school event that month, and Columbia was feeling incredibly lonely. I told her I had plans that weekend with a friend – I still hated using that word to talk about Jordan – but that if my friend – damn word – could come with me, we'd both love to check out Columbia. She said that sounded fantastic, and gave me the address for her place.

Word had reached our little town about a kid in Wyoming who had been basically crucified just for being gay earlier in the month, and Jordan and I were really shook up about it. It brought back all these feelings related to Daniel and Roger at a time when we were really getting close again, and so we were spending as much time together as we could, both for support and as we built the next version of us following his return from the church trip. As a result, there was no way I was breaking our plans to hang out that weekend even if that would have been what I wanted to do, and so the only way I was going was if Jordan wanted to get out of town too. In truth, I thought getting out of town might be good for us at that moment, and I really thought Jordan and Claire would hit it off.

"Go to Columbia to hang out with who?" Jordan asks.

"Her name is Claire, I don't think you know her. We met while you and I weren't speaking. She graduated in May, and now goes to the University of South Carolina."

"Were you and her, you know?"

"No, why?"

"I don't know, I was just curious."

"Do you think that every time I mention a new girl?"

Laughing, Jordan says, "Okay, I just realized how stupid this sounds, but I think that every time you mention anyone new."

"Glad to know my sluttiness does not stand in the way of your love."

"No way baby, I celebrate you in all your whorish glory!"

Both of us laughing, I say, "So, what do you think?"

"Sure, let's go, we've both always wanted to check out Columbia, and if you like this girl I would love to meet her."

That Saturday morning, I called and made sure Claire still wanted us to come up, and when she did, Jordan and I headed out on the Interstate. To get to Columbia, we simply went the opposite direction of Atlanta on the interstate for about 45 minutes. As we drove, we listened to a Garth Brooks album Jordan had just gotten, and talked about the trip. "So, does this person know about us?"

"No, she doesn't. She knew I was messed up over an ex and offered to listen, but I never really talked to her about it."

"Should I butch it up for the weekend?"

"Is that even something you know how to do?" Laughing, he adopts a gruff voice and starts talking about basketball saying the word chick every seven words or so and scratching his crotch. "Not bad, better than I could do, did you get that from camping with the guys." We both laugh, and I say, "No, just be you and we'll play it by ear. I don't think she would care, especially since she's really close with Charlotte, but let's be safe." I couldn't stop thinking about the kid in Wyoming, and I didn't feel like taking any chances.

"So, she's not like us, right? You know, like me or you?"

"Right, as far as I know, she's pure hetero and she has a boyfriend, his name is Devin, and he seemed pretty cool when I met him. They've been together a few years and they live together in Columbia, but he's not in town right now, some school thing."

"So, how did y'all start hanging out?"

I rub the cheek she smacked the night we met. "I went to a party with Abs, one of the blowouts on the river, and we met there and just kind of bonded right away. The same way I met Charlotte."

"I feel like I'm missing something," Jordan says, "But okay, as long as I have nothing to worry about here."

"Nothing to worry about at all." I didn't like leaving out details, but I also remembered that, like Abs, Jordan was pretty adamant about the importance of privacy.

And with that, we entered the Columbia, South Carolina metropolitan area, or at least that is what the sign said. At this point in the late 1990s, Columbia, like the city across the river from where we grew up, was more a city in name and size than appearance. It really just looked like a bunch of connecting roads, businesses and strip malls until you got to downtown. It was plenty big, but it just didn't feel urban the way Atlanta did. We followed the directions Claire had given me, and after a few road changes, we found ourselves in a neighborhood that looked like it had seen both better and worse days. Many of the houses and storefronts were in the process of renovation, and real estate signs dotted the sidewalks. It looked like it was in the process of bouncing back from hard times.

Claire's place was a little bungalow nestled alongside other similar homes on a street called Laurens not far from the college campus. As we pulled up, Claire must have spotted us from the window because she came out the front door waving. I parked the car, turned off the ignition, and turned to Jordan about to say something like let's go, but he looked like something was wrong or off or something I couldn't quite make out. He was just sitting there staring at Claire like she was the scariest monster in the history of Stephen King novels. Or maybe it wasn't fear but something else, I couldn't really tell. He just looked like he'd seen a ghost or something. I was confused. What was going on here? I said his name. He didn't respond. I grabbed his arm, he looked at me, looked back at Claire, and looked like he wanted to run as fast as he possibly could either toward or away from Claire for some reason.

While I tried to figure out what was happening, Claire reached the driver's side window, and without warning, Jordan said, "Hey CC," in a hesitant voice. Claire's eyes opened wide, took in Jordan from head to toe, looked at me, and then stared at Jordan. I was wondering what CC meant. Claire had the same dazed, I think I've seen a ghost look he did. What the hell was going on? I had heard the name CC before somewhere, but I could not place where. The two of them just stared at each other without saying a word, and then, slowly, both a little hesitant, they each started to smile. And then, they both started laughing. Okay, maybe this was a good kind of surprise? Jordan got out of the car, and Claire came around the front of the car, and they hugged each other enthusiastically. I watched all this looking forward to figuring out what the hell was going on. They both seemed to have forgotten I was there.

"Oh my god Jordan, you look great! How have you been?"

"I'm doing good, I'm a senior this year, and thinking about maybe going to college."

"That's fantastic. Wait, a minute, is he the one, you know, the one you were in love with when we were kids? Is it him?" She points at me as I make my way out of the car, and start moving toward them. When we were kids, I think? And almost as quickly, I thought, I better be the one, and kind of giggled at myself.

"Actually, yes, that's him, always has been."

"Small world, wow, small world."

"I know, so weird. I haven't seen you in years, and then you two become friends while I'm being an asshole, what are the odds."

Finally speaking up, the confusion was starting to really annoy me, I said, "Hello? Jordan, Claire, what's going on?"

"Oh shit," they both said at once, and it was kind of cute. They really had forgotten I was there for a moment. Luckily, I was too amused by the scene in front of me to be offended by this. Then, talking over, around, and in between each other, they started to explain that Claire, or CC as she was called then, had known Jordan when they were kids. They used to hang out in the diner together while Jordan's mom and CC's mom worked their shifts. CC's dad would come by and visit her there and he kind of took Jordan under his wing and would take the two kids to get ice cream or tell them all kinds of stories about his life, their moms, and his husband.

"Wait a minute," I said, "Roger is your father?" Almost immediately, my eyes went straight to the two rings she was wearing now as she did every time I had ever seen her, and my mind went back to Roger talking with the guy in the magazine shop.

Laughing, Claire says, "Yes, him and Daniel were kind of like both my dads while I was growing up, and Roger is the reason I exist." Jordan and Claire start laughing at the confusion that I am sure is obvious on my face. "I'm donor conceived. My mom could not have kids sexually for some reason, but she got hooked up with this group of doctors at the medical college who wanted her to be part of a study, and in exchange, took care of the cost of her having a child. So, wanting me to be able to know where I came from because many donor conceived children did not get to back then, she called her best friend from college, Roger. Roger agreed to do it, and him and Daniel basically treated me as their own daughter because my mom liked them being part of my life, and so they helped her raise me from the time I was born."

Speaking up, Jordan says, "She was the first one I talked to about kissing you that night at the park," and I thought, that's where I heard the name CC before. Jordan continued, "But then later that year, Roger got her mom a good job out at the plant where he worked, and she moved to the other side of town. We lost touch, but Roger would always tell me how she was doing when I visited him."

"Same thing," she says, "He would always ask me if I remembered you, and tell me about the things you were doing."

"But then after Daniel died," Jordan continues, "Roger just kind of fell apart, you saw that yourself when you and Abs ran into him, and he stopped really talking about anything but Daniel."

"He was the same way the few times I saw him. He didn't want mom or me coming by any more. He was scared someone would hurt us. He was broken, I mean, Daniel was everything to him, it was just like night and day the way he changed afterward."

It was like a family reunion. The three of us all hugged one more time, and then we headed into her bungalow, got some wine, and spent the afternoon and the evening catching up on the back porch. She told us about her college experience so far, and we told her what we were up to back home. She asked about and we told her about our relationship to that point, and all the ups and downs along the way. Mostly, though, we talked about Roger and Daniel and her mom, and the way they all were while Daniel was still around. She told me stories about Jordan as a little boy, and he told me stories about CC, the child everyone knew could do anything.

She told us that Roger was doing a little bit better. He was living down in Florida, and had met some other people that he liked down there. She told us her and her mom were planning to go visit him the next summer. She told us about donor conception, and what it was like for her. Even Jordan didn't know anything about this when they were little, but apparently, she had been told at a very early age and spent a lot of her life studying the topic. She talked about wanting to meet other kids who were donor conceived.

We told her about the latest adventures of Abs and Charlotte, and she told us about how Charlotte took care of her when she lost Daniel. She told us about Devin's trip to North Carolina and how the two of them were loving being back together and building a life at the university. He was working with other students on a healthcare project competition, and was going to call tomorrow to update her on everything going on up there. We sat there late into the night just enjoying each other's company, histories, and future plans. In the morning, the three of us went out to the flea market on the west side of the city, the biggest one I had ever seen at that point, and Jordan and I headed back home.

CHAPTER 41

"I slept with Charlotte," Abs said as I sat down on her back porch.

"I slept with Jordan," I responded with a smile.

It was a few weeks after our trip to Columbia, and Jordan and I felt like we were in a good place again. Claire and Jordan reignited their friendship from the past, and spent each day on the phone for a while, and as a result, Jordan was a lot more open and talkative than usual. He said there was something about that day in Columbia that just made things click in his head. He was tired of being scared, tired of being ashamed, he just wanted to live and enjoy life the way Roger and Daniel did. He still wanted us to keep our relationship quiet, and we agreed this was smart especially after what happened in Wyoming, but he didn't want anything to come between us.

He even softened on the idea of Lena and I maybe fooling around from time to time, but Lena had just started seeing a guy she really liked so I thought it was better that we just focus on the two of us unless it turned out that wouldn't work for me after all. I did, however, promise that I would tell him if at any point I needed to step outside of the two of us for any reason we would talk about it first so we could figure it out together. Lena and Claire both congratulated us on working through the hard times, and Abs suggested that maybe we were finally figuring things out. Life was starting to feel okay again, and I was with Abs sharing all the dirt.

"So, sex machine, how was Charlotte?"

"Did you know about strap ons? Did you know about these things and never tell me? Where was my intro to strap ons lesson that day I hung out with you, Nick and Rachel?"

"I feel like there are words missing from your questions."

"Shut up."

"Yes, I have heard of strap ons, but I have not used one so I don't know much about them. I know that Lena and I went and looked at them and she tried some on because Nick pointed out that if I ever wanted to be monogamous with a female, a strap on might come in handy in the bedroom because then I wouldn't have to choose between types of sex."

"They are fun."

"Okay."

"Charlotte and I were doing all this stuff, and it was a lot of fun, you know. We had fooled around a couple times, and I liked it, but I kind of missed, you know, that."

"Well that sounds like a good time to get a strap on."

"You know, exactly, and that's what Charlotte said, and I'm like, a what? So she told me about it, and the next time we got together we were at her house, and she pulls out this thing, you know, one of those, a green one with a little belt thing you wear, you know. And oh my god, that thing was awesome!" She starts giggling and punching me in the arm, "It was so much fun!"

"That sounds about right from what I've heard."

"Why did I never know about this? How did you know?"

"I knew about them first because Nick has a couple of them, and showed them to me. Nick liked to wear them even when he wasn't having sex. And then, Taylor explained how she uses them in the bedroom with Nick, and then Lena and I went looking at them. I didn't think to mention it to you, but I thought they were cool."

"How are Nick and Taylor?"

"They're doing great. Lena talked to them a couple weeks ago. They live by this really big lake in the heart of Orlando, and they go out walking around the lake all the time. They love it down there, and say it's a different culture than up here."

"They were always so perfect together."

"No shit, we could all take lessons from them." I light a smoke, "So, any feelings for Charlotte, or still just fun?"

"Just fun," she says, steals my cigarette, and continues, "But lots and lots of fun," and starts giggling again. "We might have to stop soon though because she met a cool goth girl who goes to the college and they might get serious. Charlotte is like nuts every time she sees this girl, and I met her the other day, and she is like mind blowing beautiful and funny. I was impressed."

"How do you feel about that?"

"Happy for Charlotte honestly. She's amazing, and she wants love and I want to see her find love, you know. I'll miss fooling around, but it would be the same thing if I fell for someone, and I wouldn't want to keep her from that, you know."

"That makes sense."

"How are you and Jordan doing?"

"We're having a lot of fun. Its not the same as last time, but it's really good. I feel like we grew a lot last year, and we're somehow even stronger together now. It's like..." but Abs gave me a signal to be quiet. I didn't know why, but then I heard the gate open, and someone came into the backyard.

"Sup losers," Zach said.

We both said hello to Zach, and both noticed that he looked different. He had bags under his eyes, and a scowl where his always-trying-to-get-laid smile used to live. He didn't look like he had cleaned his face or his clothes recently, and he smelled heavily of liquor and pot. He was just staring at us, or really at Abs, with this contemptuous look, and then he lit a cigarette and said, "Y'all seen Jordan around lately?" He kept sniffling like maybe he had a cold.

"Jordan is up in Columbia this weekend, he's hanging out with Claire," I say, and for a moment Zach looks at me, his eyes look hollow somehow and I wonder what is going on with him, but then he stares at Abs again.

"He's been up there with that chick a lot lately, hasn't he?"

Ignoring the derogatory term because with Zach there is no point in arguing about it I have learned over and over again, I say, "Well, yeah, they're really good friends and used to be really close as kids. I think they can relate to each other on a lot of levels."

"Maybe," Zach scoffs and spits into the grass. "Maybe," he says again, "Or maybe he's just tired of the shit tail here and looking to Columbia for something better." His eyes never leave Abs, and I get the distinct impression – as does Abs I learn later – that he is insulting her specifically in this moment, but I'm not sure why. One thing we all know is that Zach sees Abs as the basic personification of human perfection so this seems really strange. Zach finishes his cigarette, spits again, rubs his nose a little harder than I think seems smart, throws the cigarette in the grass instead of the ash tray on the porch, and says, "Alright," before heading out the way he came in initially. I turn to Abs, and she just shrugs.

CHAPTER 42

"I'm going to spend this weekend with Zach," Jordan says as we walk on the concrete track that once was an old railroad line. We pass our old path, and both kind of smile at the memories in these woods and the fact that you still can't really tell it was a path. Once upon a time, so much planning went into that sanctuary.

"What's going on?"

Stopping for a minute and lighting a smoke, Jordan says, "Well, you know how you said Zach seemed tense, and maybe angry, last month when he stopped by Abs' house looking for me?" I nod, and he says, "I think something might really be wrong with him. He's like that all the time lately, and it only seems to be getting worse. I don't know, I'm just worried about him so I think I should see if he will talk about whatever is going on." He kicks a leaf that falls on his shoe, "I mean, he just seems a little out of it."

"You are talking about Zach you know," I say, but Jordan doesn't find it funny. "You're really worried?"

"I really am. I mean, ever since Willow he's been a little bit erratic, even for Zach," he says as I start to comment, "But I think whatever it is has gotten worse. He barely goes to school, and when he finally shows up he starts fights with people. Hell, he's not even really chasing after Abs anymore. It's like he's giving up on everything or something. I mean, he got suspended from the basketball team for acting out, whatever that means, and he always looks disheveled when I see him. I mean, I get it, Zach's always been out there, don't say it okay, but even for him this is odd. He's not acting like himself and I think something might be really wrong. I don't know, he's never been the talker, but I gotta try."

"Well," I say, shrugging, "Then I guess you should look in on him, and hopefully you can help him. I can't really argue with you here. Even considering his usual insanity, he does seem to have gone off the deep end of late from what I saw that day, what Abs has told me, and what you're saying. I hope you can help him."

"I hope so," Jordan says staring off into the distance.

I grab his hand and we start walking again. I'm worried about Jordan. He might have the biggest heart on the planet, and as a result, I know worrying about Zach is really tearing at him inside. I don't know what might be going on with Zach, and I honestly hope this is just another example of his usual chaotic behavior, but I know it's got to be hard for Jordan. I'm thinking about this, and what I should do now that I have a weekend all to myself when Jordan says, "What are you up to the weekend before Christmas?"

Jordan knows I don't really plan that far ahead, so I wonder what is on his mind as I say, "No plans yet, what's up?"

He stops in the path again, and this time he begins shifting his feet in the way he often does when he's nervous. "There is a dance in Columbia. Claire and I found out about it when I was up there the other week. I was thinking, maybe, if you want to, maybe we could go to it, maybe together?"

I pull him too me, softly kiss him, and say, "I would love to go to a dance with you. I'll even dress up if you want me to."

He kisses me back, and says, "Really?"

"Yeah, it should be fun. What's the dance for?"

"A student group up there, a group of people like us, and the church up there like the one I go to are putting it on. It's supposed to be like a winter celebration or something, but I just thought it would be cool to be at a dance where we could actually dance." He blushes just a little bit, and I kiss him again.

"That sounds like fun to me. Are Claire and Devin going? Or is it only for people like us?" Jordan got to meet Devin on his last visit, and like everyone else, fell in love with the guy on the spot.

"They were going to come with us, and maybe Charlotte, but we could just go the two of us if you want, or whatever."

He's so cute when he's nervous. "I think the idea of all of us going together sounds great. It should be a lot of fun, and you're really cute right now," I say and kiss him again. He blushes a little more, grabs my hand, and starts walking.

That weekend, Jordan goes off with Zach and stays at Zach's house all weekend. He doesn't find out what is up with Zach, but when I meet up with the two of them Monday afternoon Zach does seem a little more relaxed. I spend my weekend down at the river writing in my latest journal and riding through the countryside with an ecstatic Abs who just got accepted into her first choice college via early admission. We spend the latter part of the weekend celebrating, and dreaming about the coming years.

CHAPTER 43

"Are you ready for the big dance silly?" Lena asks walking up to me on a corner in Milledgeville, Georgia. It is the weekend before the dance, and Lena invited me to come up here because we just had to check out this bookstore and catch up.

"I'm as ready as I'll ever be."

Like Jordan, Lena knows full well that I'm not the most social person, but we both also know that dancing out with other people without fear will mean the world to Jordan. Simply put, I'm going to a dance. Lena has added a nose ring to her ensemble, and she is bouncing up and down as we move through town toward the bookstore. The town is like so many I will see over the years throughout the southeast. Almost nothing nearby, a handful of nice neighborhoods beside less nice neighborhoods, and a downtown area that looks like something out of an old television show.

"You will have so much fun, and it will make Jordan's year," she says as she pulls me into a coffee shop at the last possible second before we walk past it. "It's going to be beautiful, and if you take pictures, I so want one." I assure her that if there are souvenirs one will have her name on it, and we order coffees and take a seat outside of the shop. "So silly, how are things with you and Jordan?"

"Things are," I pause smiling and blushing and she giggles, "Really good. Things are great, fun again, you know, we're back in sync as your mom would say."

"That's great! Where is he this weekend?"

"He is hanging out with Zach. He is worried about Zach, and thinks Zach might be in some real trouble. I don't know. I'm glad he cares so much, but I just don't really know what's going on."

"Well, and you know I'm right so don't bother arguing, you love how caring Jordan is, and you wouldn't change it for the world so this is that part of him at work. Plus, whatever is going on with Zach, if anyone can help, it will be Jordan. Let's not forget that I was once a troubled young lass everyone was worried about. I'm sure Jordan knows what he is doing."

"You are right on all points."

"I usually am," she says and sticks her tongue out at me, which also now has a piercing in it, a cute little ball of a thing that kind of reaches out at you each time she opens her mouth.

"I like the jewelry, what happened to your aversion to it?"

"Body jewelry is different than other jewelry, body jewelry I like. They are kind of cool. I also got my first tattoo."

"Really, what did you get?"

She stands up, pulls her jeans down just a little bit and raises her shirt. There, just under her waistline near her hipbone, she now has what looks like a Chinese symbol on her body. It has a certain charm to it, but I have no clue what it means. I sit there staring at it for a little while thinking about just how perfectly it seems to fill the space. "What do you think," she asks with a big grin on her face.

"I think its really pretty," I say, "But I don't know what it means."

"Its Chinese, or Mandarin, I'm not sure the difference actually. Anyway, it means perseverance."

"Now, that fits you."

"I know! I love it!"

"So what made you finally decide to do the body art thing?"

"I don't really know. I'd talked about it for so long and I just woke up one morning, and thought, it's time to just do it."

"Makes a lot of sense to me, I mean, you've known you wanted a tattoo since I was 10 I think, and you were always curious about body piercings after you dated that guy, what was his name, the one with all the piercings?"

"Mitch, ah Mitch, he was so sweet and stupid, but he had great art and he really knew how to use his tongue, good ole Mitch."

"Yep, that's him, Mitch. Speaking of guys, how are things with Derrick?"

"Over and never going to start again for even a second."

"Already? What did he do?"

"He did not get along with Greg, and I think you know what I mean."

"Asshole."

"Exactly, I sent his homophobic ass packing. Too bad too, he had a nice body." With that, she grabs my hand, and we are off again. We go by the bookstore, and I find myself wondering what the point of the trip was since it is nothing special. I mean, we could get the same thing in my city or hers. A few years later, an old firehouse in the town will be turned into a bookstore with coffee and a lot of books not common in the small town book stores I've visited for years, but at this point, we are visiting just another room full of books without much to recommend it. Then again, I thought, this is Lena so maybe there was no real reason for the trip other than hanging out for a little while. We spend an hour in the bookstore and while we're there I pick up a Stephen King novel I know Jordan hasn't read yet. Then, after having exhausted the tiny space of the shop, Lena says, "Well, I should start heading back, but first, you need to come to my car silly."

I don't bother asking why. There is really no point. She'll only tell me if she wants to. We walk back to Lena's car. She tells me to close my eyes, and when I do, she opens the trunk. After a few seconds and some sounds I cannot place, she tells me to open them. I do, and I see my three favorite skirts that normally live in her closet in Atlanta. "What is this," I ask.

"They're for you silly, you can pick one to wear to the dance." She smiles really big the same way she did last time she ambushed me right before a party. "Jordan called me, and we both agreed that since y'all would be in a safe space, you should have the chance to choose whether or not you wanted to wear one of your skirts to the dance. So, here are the ones you like the most just in case you want to wear one next weekend."

I stand there smiling at Lena, and feeling touched that her and Jordan set this up behind my back. I pick the pink one, and then I take the red one too. She laughs, and I say I'll decide when the time comes. She giggles, and tells me that is exactly what she would do. We embrace, and she tells me to call her when I get home so she knows I'm safe. I smile as she drives away, holding the bag that hides the two skirts I will pick between for the dance the following weekend. For a minute, I look around the town, and wonder just how similar or different it is from my own. Holding my bag close to my chest, I walk over to my car, and head back to South Carolina.

CHAPTER 44

"Welcome to the ball you all," a short young man says as we enter the auditorium hosting the dance the Saturday night before Christmas. Our senior year is halfway over, Jordan is eighteen years old, and Abs and I will catch up on him age-wise in a couple months. We walk into the dance smiling at the rainbow decorations and the sound of Brandy and Monica's "The boy is mine." Everywhere, people are dancing, talking, and just hanging out at tables or over by the food. It feels like a good night.

I decide to wear the red skirt, and I have matched it with a black button down shirt that goes well with the black pants and red button down shirt Jordan is wearing. We stand there holding hands watching the scene in front of us. To our right, Abs and Charlotte are dressed in matching silk blue shirts and black pants – at Charlotte's request – and pointing at the photo booth across the room. On our left, Claire and Devin are standing together holding hands and jokingly half-dancing to the music already. Claire chose a beautiful purple dress that accentuates her figure, and goes well with the purple shirt Devin wears over a pair of black pants. Standing there together, the six of us all feel like the belles of the ball.

After a few seconds, a photographer comes up and asks if we want a group photo. We say yes, take the photo, and give him the bungalow address to send the pictures we purchase. Since all of us are staying at the bungalow, we decided ahead of time to go our own ways, and stay as long as we wanted on our own tonight. Without a word, after the group photo, we break into three little groups. Claire and Devin head for the dance floor, and can be seen there together dancing with each other and lots of others the rest of the night. Abs and Charlotte head for the photo booth, and in the coming weeks we will all be shown the hilarity that ensued in their four straight rounds of photos over and over again.

Jordan and I move more slowly than the other two groups. Instead of running off from the spot we stand in, he turns to me and kisses me in front of the whole crowd. There are no insults coming, no taunts, no bullshit. Instead, we hear people clapping and a couple others cheering as we stand there kissing in the front of the room like something out of a movie. When our lips finally part, he leads me to the dance floor, and as Shania Twain's "You're still the one" starts to play, we dance, together, in our own private moment surrounded by other people. The music plays and stops, but we just keep moving together feeling each other, feeling the night, and feeling a sense of freedom that cannot be put into words.

As the night continued, our little group came back together and separated again a few different times, but Jordan and I stayed almost glued to each other throughout. I kept thinking about my birthday years before, and the ways the cigarettes and wine scent littered the candle lit room. I kept thinking of rolling in the grass with him when we were kids. I kept thinking of the long road we took to get to this dance, and these moments with good friends, music, and public displays of affection. We played around in the photo booth. We got food at the table on the side of the auditorium. We both took turns dancing with Abs and Claire and Devin and Charlotte, but we mostly danced with each other. We went outside a couple times for smokes. We laughed at the antics of others, cheered at the other couples having a free night out, and chanted with the rest of the crowd when the disc jockey told us to.

Later in the night, Jordan and I were standing over by one of the walls when we were greeted by a face I had not seen in a very long time. What's his name came walking over to me holding hands with Lenny, yep, that Lenny, and said, "Hey."

"Hi," I said happy to see him smiling and holding hands with someone who – despite my well-earned hatred for – was by all accounts a decent guy.

"I wanted to say I was sorry. We both did actually." Lenny blushed, and looked at the floor. I took a little bit of satisfaction from that, which I'm not sure if I am proud of to this day.

Jordan started to speak, but I stopped him, placing my hand on his chest. I knew that he still held even more negative feelings for these two than I did, and I thought tonight was a night for rising above such things. I smiled at Jordan, he nodded, and I said, "Don't worry about it mate, let's face it, growing up different is simply a shit show, and we all did things we're not proud of along the way." Lenny, what's his name, and most importantly Jordan all smiled, and the three of us stood there talking for a few more minutes. Lenny was getting ready to go to Tennessee for college, and what's his name was planning to go with him and finish high school there. They had been seeing each other for about four months, and something I actually am proud of to this day, they had seen our relationship as a kind of model for creating a healthy one for themselves. I didn't have the heart to tell them just how much Jordan and I put each other through so I just took the compliment, grabbed Jordan, and went back out on the dance floor where the rest of our group was engaged in a mass slow dance.

As the official ending of the event drew closer, Abs and Charlotte came bouncing up to the rest of us grinning like they had just won the lottery. Apparently, they had. Giggling with Charlotte, Abs said, "We met the most amazing people out back while we were smoking, and we're going to go to an after party over in Forest Hills with them."

Charlotte piped up, "We hit the jackpot! One of the girls came with her sister because she was nervous about coming alone, and she is crazy about Abs!"

"And the other sister is nuts about Charlotte," Abs said and they both started giggling again.

"Do you have your phone Abs," I asked, and Abs nodded and pulled it out of her purse. She was the first one in our group to have a cellular telephone, and I thought maybe this was the perfect situation for those things. "Have fun y'all," I said, and they looked at Claire who nodded before they almost bounced away to a couple of sisters waiting across the room.

"Y'all ever wonder where those two get so much energy," Devin asks with a chuckle and we all nod and laugh along with him. "What about you two," he asks with a smile.

I look at Jordan, who says, "We're going to go off on our own for the rest of the night," which is a surprise to me, but a welcome one. Jordan apparently booked us a hotel room not far from the event so we could spend the night together without any distractions, concerns, or clothes.

CHAPTER 45

When I woke up the next morning, Jordan was sleeping peacefully with his head on my chest. Our clothes were all over by the floor, and I felt all the right kinds of sore. I had to get up to go to the restroom so I softly moved his head onto a pillow, and rolled out of bed. When I came back into the room, I brewed a cup of coffee, lit a cigarette, and sat in the armchair where I could watch him sleep.

He was sound asleep. After leaving the dance, we walked around downtown for a little while talking about the night. It was then he told me about the hotel room as we stood right across the street from it. Together, we went inside, and went to our room. We spent the night making love, and fell asleep wrapped in each others' arms – immersed in what felt like the most perfect of nights. As I took my seat in the armchair, I just kind of smiled at the sight of him there in the bed. I tried to memorize the scene so I could play it over and over again in my head in the years to come, feel this alive and free again whenever I needed to.

I sat there for a long time. I could see his left leg peaking out from underneath the covers, straddling the covers just a little bit, and something about that image just made me want to never close my eyes. The top part of his back was exposed to the light, and his breathing provided a soundtrack for my visual odyssey that morning. I smoked my cigarette and thought about the way his body felt the night before on the dance floor, in the bedroom, and I just let the little bit of sunlight coming through the blinds wash over me. I thought about him kissing me in front of everyone at the dance. I sat there and wondered if it was possible for life to get any better.

I looked at the clock, and saw it was around 11 in the morning. Jordan booked the room for two nights so there was no need to worry about checking out, but I wanted to check in on Abs. I put on a pair of jeans and a t-shirt I had in my book bag, and stepped out into the hallway. It was the typical hotel hallway with muted colors, and odd little patterns on the carpet. I spotted a sign that pointed toward the lobby, and I figured they would likely have a phone I could use there.

I walked down to the lobby, and called Abs on her cellular phone. She answered on the second ring, and I said, "Hey, you doing okay? I just wanted to check in."

"Yeah," she said sighing softly and from the sound of it, exhaling smoke. "We made it back to the house around 5 in the morning and slept in the guest bedroom. Where did y'all go?"

"Jordan got us a hotel room near the dance. Five in the morning, what are you doing up?"

"I was just having a smoke after using the bathroom and the phone rang."

"Well go back to sleep, and we'll talk later. I just wanted to make sure you were okay."

"Love y'all."

"We love you too Abs."

I hung up the courtesy phone, and thanked the lady behind the counter for letting me use it. A few years later, I would go in hotels and be surprised not to see public phones anymore, but of course, by then most of us would be carrying little computers in our pockets everywhere we went. I stepped out into the sunlight, and just let it bathe me for a second. The streets were already alive with people likely going to churches, brunches, walks in the park, and other Sunday morning activities around the city. The coffee in the hotel, as is often the case, wasn't very good so I decided to take a quick stroll to what looked like a coffee stand in the building next door, and pick up one of the fancy coffees Jordan liked, and a better cup than I could get at the hotel for me.

When I got back to the room, Jordan was stirring in the bed. I handed him the drink I picked up at the shop, and crawled into bed with him. I lit us both cigarettes, and we just stayed there enjoying the morning for a little while. After a few cigarettes and kisses, we took a long hot shower, and got dressed. Around six that evening, we headed back over to the bungalow, picked up Abs and Charlotte, and headed back to our little town.

CHAPTER 46

"Happy birthday beautiful" Abs yelled as I walked through the gate, and took the hug she was offering and my spot on her back porch.

Christmas and New Years passed in a blur of activity, and our last semester of high school had come right onto center stage. Jordan and I were moving forward full speed ahead both looking for jobs and applying to colleges in Atlanta, and planning our future with each day we got closer to graduation. Abs had been hanging out a lot with Charlotte, and her new girlfriend Marcy who also happened to be the sister of Charlotte's new girlfriend Mandy. After meeting at the dance, the four of them spent the past couple months going back and forth to see each other here and in Columbia. Claire proposed to Devin on New Year's Eve, and he said yes. They were planning a small wedding in the summer, and continuing their work at the university. Even Zach started coming back around again with Jordan, though he still seemed tense and a little off most of the time and Jordan was still worried about him.

"My birthday was Tuesday my dear."

"But I didn't see you outside of school until now, so today is your birthday in my world," Abs said smiling, pouring two glasses of wine, and handing me a little box shaped thing wrapped in Winnie the Pooh paper.

"What is this?"

"Open it and find out."

Lena made the Dean's list at her school at the end of the fall semester, and was starting to get a couple acoustic gigs here and there around her neighborhood. She was also starting to play with a band that recently had to shake up their lineup, and bringing in a little cash in the process. She called me on my birthday, and promised me any record I wanted next time I came to Atlanta. She was in between lovers again, as she put it, but her and Greg decided, after his latest boyfriend proved as useless as the rest, that they would just say screw it, get drunk, and make music on their own for the rest of their lives. They both had new apartments again, and were once again neighbors like when they lived off Moreland Avenue so this sounded like a realistic plan to me.

"Okay," I said as I pulled the paper off the box to reveal a copy of the latest Ani DeFranco record, and squealed with delight exclaiming, "Thank you thank you thank you Abs!"

Abs giggled at my reaction, lit a smoke, and said, "So did you hear from any colleges yet?"

I had not heard from any colleges yet, but I also only applied to the ones in Atlanta, and they all said I should expect something later in the spring. I already decided – though Abs didn't like it – that I was going to Atlanta after graduation with or without college. I would figure out stuff later if I needed to, but at that moment, I just wanted to go experience the city I spent so much time dreaming about in the past couple years.

"Nope, but I'm not worried about it. You looking forward to moving?"

"You know it."

"It's going to be strange not to be right down the road from each other."

"Yep," she says, flicks an ash from her smoke, "But you better damn well visit or I'll hunt you down." She grins at me, but I'm pretty sure she's actually serious about this.

"I will, and you'll be welcome wherever we settle in Atlanta." Where exactly that would be was a whole other question. At present, the plan was for Jordan, Lena, Greg, and I to try to rent a house together that was situated near a train station so we could pool our resources and have more money for other things. Greg and Lena were already on the lookout for places, and Jordan was sure they would find a good one, though I was less optimistic after witnessing their repeated moves over the past couple years.

"Hey, where is Jordan, I thought he was coming by tonight?"

"He is," I said blowing out a puff of smoke and taking a sip of my wine. "He wanted to check in on Zach first so he'll probably be by in a little bit."

"How is Zach doing?"

"I don't know. Jordan is still worried about him. He thinks Zach is into both drugs and alcohol more than he will admit, and he still thinks something is going on that we don't know about. At the same time, Jordan is very protective, and Zach has been coming around from time to time lately, so who knows."

"Is he still planning to join the military?"

"Was there ever any other option," I ask, surprised.

"I didn't think so," she says sighing, "But Mikey down at the garage, you know the guy Lindsey's been seeing, he said Zach was over there trying to get a job and not a part time job but a full time one so I wasn't sure."

"I didn't know anything about that. As far as I know, Zach is still all about the military." I really didn't know anything about the situation, but now I was a little worried. Zach never wavered in his plans, it was his one consistent quality, and so why was he looking for other work all of the sudden? I decided I should tell Jordan about this little detail just in case it mattered. At the same time, I started wondering what was going on up at Zach's. Jordan wanted to stop by because he said Zach was all alone at the house this weekend, but I started to wonder if maybe I should have gone with him.

"You okay over there," Abs asks.

"Yeah, just thinking about this little town and all that has happened here. It's kind of funny to think about this place without us, but I honestly can't wait to get out of here."

"I feel the same way. This place had its good points, but I think we kind of outgrew it, you know, and that feels like a good thing to me."

"Me too," I say smiling at Abs. We might have outgrown this place, but not each other. Wherever we go from here, I know that we'll always be in touch. "Speaking of things that you outgrow, did I tell you Jordan and I ran into what's his name?"

"No you didn't? What was that like?"

"He was at the dance back in December, and he was there with Lenny and they're a couple now. They're very happy and moving to Tennessee to build a life together"

"Oh shit, how did I miss this?"

"You were probably out back getting to know Marcy's intimate details."

She punches me in the arm, and says, "Probably."

"Then why punch me," I ask.

"Old habits man, old habits. So, what happened and why am I only hearing about this now, I mean, come on you're slipping on your news coverage old man?"

"No real reason, I mean, there wasn't much to tell. They walked up to Jordan and I and apologized for the past. It was actually kind of nice, and then the four of us just stood there and chatted for a while. They really seemed to be doing well, and for some reason, I kind of like that they are, regardless of the past."

"Wow, that's actually pretty cool. Damn, I guess things do change after all. Ooh, speaking of things that change, did you hear about your old friend Becca?"

"Nope, what happened now?"

"She didn't come back to school after winter break."

"What?"

"Word is, she got pregnant by some guy at the church, and the two of them ran off over the holidays to avoid facing their parents. Lindsey said she saw them loading up his car the day before Christmas, and no one has seen them since. Lindsey thought the guy had some family out in Texas, somewhere around Liberty she thought she'd heard, and so she's guessing that's where they went."

"Holy shit."

"I know right? Little miss better than everybody – one of the good kids, you know – just damn fell apart right out of nowhere."

"Wow, I bet the church is in flames with all the gossip this has to be generating."

We both laugh at the thought for a few seconds, and Abs goes, "Well, you know the church folk love a good story."

"Ain't that the truth," I say and we both start laughing again as I add, in my best Southern Belle accent, "Well bless her heart."

Sitting on the back porch where we spent so many nights, laughing like a couple kids who have been laughing at and with each other all their lives, I found myself smiling about just how fast some things change, and just how constant other things remain.

CHAPTER 47

Around 11 o'clock that night, I started really wondering what was keeping Jordan. I decided I would walk up to Zach's house to see what was going on. It was only a couple blocks, I really missed Jordan, and it was a nice night so I thought what the hell. Abs offered to go with me, but I told her I would rather just go on by myself, and maybe Jordan and I would swing by later if it wasn't too late. Abs told me to make sure I let her know everything was okay, and then disappeared into her house. She didn't wait for a response, we were way past that in our relationship. She knew I would check in later, and tell her everything.

The neighborhood was dark and quiet. From Abs' house, Zach's place was two blocks straight out of the driveway and up the hill. I stood at the top of Abs' driveway, and lit a smoke. The crickets were singing, and I could kind of feel their song inside me. Everywhere around me, all was peaceful and easy, just like my life had become in the past few months. Something about the songs the animals were singing felt comforting so I just stood there for a few minutes smoking my cigarette and day – or night I guess – dreaming. I started walking up the hill thinking about how much fun Lena and I would have playing dress up, and how much I was sure Jordan would love Atlanta. I walked past the ranch style houses on the street, and thought about the things I already had planned for next year.

I had taken the time to make sure there were options for Jordan in case he wanted to continue to go to church, and I found a really nice church affiliated – loosely – with the one he already went to here. As I walked through the intersection halfway up the hill, I thought about the pictures of that church, and hoped Jordan would like it. I also found a couple bookstores that advertised massive collections of horror and thriller novels like the ones Jordan was always reading, and a handful of restaurants – including some suggested by Lena – that I thought might be fun for us to try. I was running through the list in my head when I arrived at Zach's house.

Even though they never seemed to lock it, I never felt comfortable just walking through the front door of Zach's house unannounced. I knocked on the door, but I didn't hear anything, and after a few minutes no one came to answer. This was not unusual since Zach spent most of the time in the basement he converted into a kind of apartment the first year he lived here. I checked the door, and as usual, it was unlocked. I walked inside the house for the first time in quite a while, and called both Zach and Jordan's names a couple times. There was no response, but I knew from experience that if they were in the basement, they probably couldn't hear me unless I screamed for them. I was never much of a screamer.

Instead, I figured I would look around, like usual, and then check out the basement. Sure enough, there was no one upstairs, and there was no one in the backyard. Since the den upstairs and the back yard were basically the only parts of the house Zach really used beyond the basement, the process of elimination said they were in the basement and hadn't heard me yet. Chuckling, I thought about the time Zach slammed the basement door scaring the hell out of all of us inside, and considered a similar prank for a few seconds. It would be hilarious, but if Zach was already having a rough time, scaring him might not be the best way to show friendship or support at the moment. I told myself, maybe next time, and headed toward the reinforced door that led down into the basement.

I remembered when Zach first moved into the area, and I was so jealous of this house. Because of the way it was structured, Zach basically had both the ultimate level of privacy – basically his own apartment – in the basement, and the ability to do whatever he wanted down there without anyone hearing or otherwise noticing. As a teenager, that kind of privacy seemed invaluable, and I wished I had it instead of Zach or anyone else for that matter. I remember Abs testing out the privacy, as she put it, by seeing just how loud they could have sex in the basement when Zach's parents were home. I doubt Zach knew about the details of that experiment, but from what I heard, he definitely enjoyed the results. More importantly, the basement wall of silence held firm best Abs could tell because they were never interrupted no matter how loud they got. Chuckling at the thought, I opened the basement door.

The door to the basement, once opened, exposed a set of stairs that wound down in a swirling fashion to the rooms below. Rather than a single room, the basement actually had four distinct components. First, there was a bedroom in the back corner where Zach slept, and that might have been used as an apartment at some point in the house's history. Second, their was a bathroom adjacent to the bedroom, which had a full tub and toilet combo as well as a fairly fancy sink Zach was pretty sure was added when the house was being put on the market the time his family bought it. Third, there was a workroom that was located on the same back wall of the house that the bedroom and bathroom occupied, and contained a built in tool bench, which Zach used for VHS movies and records because his dad had a shed in the backyard he used for tools and for a working – or drinking liquor – alone.

Finally, there was a main room that was set up much like a living room in any house. This was the room the stairs led into, and you could only access the other rooms from the doors that led to them from this main room. Zach turned the main room into what he called his party room by putting two beat up old couches, an old coffee table, and his entertainment center in it so people could hang out there when they visited. As I walked down the stairs, I thought about how rarely I had been in this space despite knowing Zach for years. I smelled what seemed like an odd mixture of body odor, mildew, stale pot, stale cigarettes, various types of alcohol, lubricants, copper, and something burnt. My eyes burned a little bit, and I wondered what the hell they were doing down there.

I got to the bottom of the steps, turned toward the main room, and I screamed and screamed and screamed.

CHAPTER 48

I don't know how long I screamed at the sight of Jordan in the middle of the room in a puddle of blood. I didn't even hear or see Zach as I finally gained control of my body and ran toward Jordan kicking a gun that was somewhere on the floor in the process. I fell into the blood, my knees covered in sticky hell, and pulled Jordan into my arms still screaming and begging him to wake up, please wake up baby, just wake the fuck up! I just sat there on the floor with him, I couldn't move or think, I just kept screaming.

A couple days after that night, a notebook arrived in the mail at Abs' house. Before she handed it over to the police, Abs made a copy of it. She read it cover to cover, and then sent it to me. It was a suicide note. It was written in Zach's handwriting. It was a documentation of his personal hell. It was the "There is something we don't know," Jordan was so sure existed. It also contained the piece of information that likely drove Zach over the edge. He failed qualification for military service and his way out of that house.

A few weeks later, Abs also sent me a copy of the official police report. According to the police report, Zach's body showed evidence of extensive, long term, physical and sexual abuse. The medical examiners estimated that he had been regularly beaten and occasionally beaten and raped since he was around 5 – 7 years old.

In the notebook, Zach wrote about his father coming to see him for "special" time when he was a little child. He wrote about being locked in the closet whenever he needed to learn to respect his father. He wrote about being beaten with boards when his father had too much to drink. He wrote about nightmares where his father choked him with something down there. He wrote about being beaten until he passed out after he cried in response to losing a basketball game. He wrote about being hit by a wrench when he needed extra "training." He wrote about the time he tried to tell on his father, and how his mother told his father everything he said, and then went in her room, out of sight, while his father taught him a lesson about talking out of turn and how well he learned that lesson.

According to the police report, I was screaming when they arrived, but I wouldn't let go of Jordan's body. They had to pry me off of him, and I apparently injured an officer in the process, but I don't remember that. Abs had gotten worried, it seemed, because she was listed as the person who called 911.

In the notebook, Zach told Abs he was sorry for giving up, and asked her to tell Jordan and I the same. He wrote about his time with us as the happiest in his life, and he wrote about how much he loved Abs and how scared that made him because he didn't want to become like his father. He wrote about Jordan, the first real friend he felt like he ever had, and how Abs needed to look out for Jordan after he was gone. He apologized for the reckless and mean things he did, and wrote about how he often did not know what he was doing because he couldn't remember the last time he slept without nightmares. He told her that he couldn't take it anymore, and that the military wouldn't take him so he needed another way out.

According to the police report, Zach's body was on the other side of the stairs when I arrived on the scene. I didn't see Zach's body. I didn't know he was there. I never noticed him. All I saw was Jordan in the middle of the room and the world fell apart.

In the notebook, Zach wrote about the summer we all seemed to drift apart, and the time he spent with Willow and her friends. He wrote about how he got hooked on cocaine and that cocaine made his drinking worse. He told her he never actually stopped doing cocaine, but just learned to hide it because he knew it scared Jordan. He wrote about how alone he felt, and how worthless he thought he was because his own parents couldn't love him. He wrote about locking himself in the basement and getting trashed after failing the military exams. He wrote about how scared he was of his father finding out he failed the military exams.

According to the police report, Jordan's death was an accident. Zach had been planning to kill himself that night. He was planning to use his gun to end his pain, but Jordan, the evidence suggested, interrupted and probably tried to save him, but the gun went off in Zach's incredibly drunk and high on cocaine hands killing Jordan almost instantly.

In the notebook, he wrote about Jordan a lot. Jordan was apparently the best thing that ever entered Zach's life. The only thing he didn't like about Jordan at first was that he had to put up with me, but even I became important to him over time. He thought Jordan was perfect, and he wanted to be more like Jordan. He wrote about how he tried to keep Jordan around him as much as possible because somehow Jordan's presence gave him hope. He wrote that Abs could show the notebook to Jordan if she thought it was the right thing to do. He wrote about Abs and Jordan as the only truly wonderful people – the only real friends – he ever encountered, and apologized for letting them down. He wrote that he hoped I would take care of them after he was gone.

According to the police report, Zach likely picked up the gun at some point – the estimate was 45 minutes after Jordan was shot or 15 minutes before I arrived at the house by my count – and ended his own life while Jordan was lying in a pool of blood a few feet away.

In the notebook, he wrote about the pain he was in. He talked about his body hurting all the time, and the cocaine and alcohol having less and less of an effect no matter how much he did. He wrote about his mind feeling like a cage, and the nightmares that would not stop for days or even weeks at a time. He wrote about his fear that he was getting worse. He wrote about, in the midst of a drunken rage, beating up a stranger outside a diner in the city, but then not being sure if that really happened or not. He wrote about just wanting the pain to end, or even to stop for just a little bit, his final words in the notebook were, "I just want it to be over."

According to the police report, I was officially cleared of any suspected involvement.

I didn't know any of this at the time. I'm not even sure if I could have told you my name in that moment. All I could feel was pain swallowing me, Jordan's crumpled body in my arms, and a sincere desire to burn down the world and everything in it. I screamed and held the love of my life until the police came, but I still don't remember much of anything after I turned around and saw Jordan on the floor in a pool of blood.

CHAPTER 49

I didn't stay for the funeral. I didn't want to say goodbye with other people who knew Jordan. I didn't want to spend another minute in the town where he died. I might have been in shock. I might have just been too sad to think. I might have just been angry. I might have been suicidal myself. I might have not been thinking straight. I don't really know how I felt, but I didn't stay for the funeral.

The police let me leave the scene early that morning. My parents were there, and they took me home. They kept saying they were sorry about my friends. More than ever, I hated that word. The moment I got home, I locked myself in my room and began packing. I kept hearing the phone in the house ringing, news was probably spreading around town, but I didn't want to talk to anyone. I wanted to talk to Jordan. I wanted to hold Jordan. I couldn't do either of those things so I just packed my stuff and hid in my room all day.

I put together all the money I had, and all the clothes I wanted to keep that I thought would fit in my trunk. When I finally took off the shirt the police had given me that morning, I put on one of Jordan's old shirts that I used to sleep in and just stared at the wall. I only wore Jordan's shirts for the next few weeks, and I remember crying when the last one finally started to fall apart later on. I kept waiting to wake up, but it didn't happen. I didn't actually sleep at all for a little while. I put together all the stuff that would fit in my car, and that night, after my parents were asleep, I loaded up everything. I sat on the back porch, and wrote my parents a letter saying I was leaving and I wasn't coming back if I could help it.

In the letter, I told them Jordan wasn't just my friend. I told them how I felt about him and how he felt about me. I told them I didn't know where I was going even though this was a lie. I lied because I didn't want to be found or even searched for at all. I lied because I wasn't sure if I would still be alive by the end of the day. I lied because I just wanted to disappear. I told them I appreciated everything good they ever did for me, and I meant it. I told them I loved them, and I think I meant that too. Ultimately, I told them goodbye for the last time to date.

As the sun rose, I pulled out of the driveway, and drove away from the house where I grew up falling in love with Jordan. I drove the two blocks to Abs' house. I went around to the back porch, and left her a much more detailed letter I wrote after I finished the one for my parents. I told her I felt like I would die if I didn't get out of here, and I told her where and how to find me and that I would be in touch as soon as I felt able. I told her I didn't know what I would do about school, but that she should try not to worry. Abs would later inform me that she was sad but not surprised when she woke up that morning and found the note. She would also later tell me that she thought she would have done the same if she had been in my shoes and seen what I had seen that night. She wasn't mad at me, and when I called her three days later she made this fact crystal clear.

After I left Abs' house, I drove to our spot – Jordan's and mine – one last time. I walked through the fields, and stood in the grass under the tree. I cried more than I expected, and cursed more than was likely useful. Part of me expected him to walk up any moment, and ask me what I was doing, but the rest of me could already begin to feel that he was gone and the numbness and shock were starting to fade. I stood there long enough to drink one more glass of wine, and have one more cigarette like we did so many times in so many places over the past decade of our lives together. Before I left the spot, I whispered, "I love you, and I always will," just in case his God really existed and might relay the message.

From the park, I drove over to Jordan's house, and sat on the curb for a few minutes just watching the place. I could see movement inside, and I figured that meant his mom was home. I debated whether or not to knock on the door for about three cigarettes, and ultimately decided that I should because I didn't know if I would ever have another chance. I could not imagine what this morning might be like for Jordan's mom, and maybe I should have cared more about that, but I did not. I wanted to say goodbye, and so I walked up to the front door and knocked on it for the last time.

She answered the door looking about as messed up as I felt inside and maybe looked on the outside, I don't know, and said, "Oh, I thought I might see you."

I asked her if I could see his room, and she said yes. I walked through the house I spent so much time in feeling like the walls were closing in on me, and made my way to Jordan's bedroom. I sat on Jordan's bed, and stayed there about thirty minutes soaking in the smell of cigarettes and wine that always consumed the house, and thinking about all the important moments in my life that took place under this roof. I remembered our first night in bed together, and our big blow out over Lenny. I remembered dancing around in the living room to a new record last week, and dancing around to what was now considered a classic record almost ten years ago. I closed my eyes as tight as I could, and for a second I could almost hear his voice, taste his lips, feel his presence, and see him in front of me. I tried to hang on to those sensations, but my eyes fell open and I was sitting there alone. Once again, just in case, I whispered, "I love you and I always will."

As I came out of the room, Jordan's mom said, "You know, you were his best friend. You meant a whole lot to him."

At first I just nodded and kept walking, but then something inside me that felt beyond my control made me turn around, and I said, "No, I was his boyfriend, and I love him and he loved me. We were together for the last ten years. He was my first kiss. We made love and laughed and cried and shared our life together. I was not just his best friend, I was his everything, and he was mine."

She stood there staring at me with more hatred than I'd ever seen in anyone's eyes before, and screamed, "Get the hell out of my house! How dare you say such evil things about my son at a time like this, you should be ashamed of yourself!"

Suddenly fearless, I simply said, "And now I know why he never wanted you to know who he really was or what we had."

Striking with the speed of a snake she slapped me hard across my face, and began screaming, "GET OUT GET OUT GET OUT," and didn't stop until I was already back at my car across the street. I got in my car, cranked up my stereo, and hit the road.

A couple hours later, I stopped at an exit on the Interstate a little over halfway to Atlanta. The exit sign said it had a gas station, and I needed to use the restroom and stretch my legs. There was nothing at the exit on the side I pulled off on except the gas station. I went to the restroom, bought a bottle of water, and picked up a fresh pack of cigarettes – legally for the first time. I wasn't ready to get back in the car so I lit a smoke, and walked around the back of the building. There was a bit of a cliff of red Georgia clay behind the station that dropped off into some woods about 500 yards down the hill. A few years later, it would hold part of a Home Depot, but it was just empty that day. As I smoked my cigarette, I considered whether or not the fall would put me out of my misery, but ultimately decided I wasn't ready to let go just yet.

I went to the car and got back on the road. I took my time on the Interstate, and arrived a couple hours later in the only place it made sense for me to go after everything that happened. I got out of the car, lit a smoke, and walked across the parking lot to the apartment building across the street. I slowly climbed a set of iron stairs to the second floor, and then to the third floor. I looked back at my car and realized I wasn't sure if I wanted to keep living or not. If I'm honest, I'm still not sure today. As I do now, however, in that moment I decided to keep going for a little while longer just in case it was worth it.

I turned around, away from the railing and the parking lots below, and knocked on the door of the apartment. As the door opened, I was met with the familiar mingling of cigarettes and wine in the air, and I heard Lena say, "Oh my god silly, I was wondering where you were" as I collapsed in the doorway, into her arms, and, for a few moments of exhaustion induced sleep, out of the pain rushing through my body since the moment I found Jordan's body.

SUGGESTED CLASS ROOM OR BOOK CLUB USE

DISCUSSION AND HOME WORK QUESTIONS

1. *Cigarettes & Wine* reveals many ways people, places, and narratives shape who we become. What are some ways external social forces shaped the lives of the characters? What are some ways social forces may have shaped you or your loved ones?

2. The vast majority of the characters in *Cigarettes & Wine* feel sexual and/or gender desires (i.e., bisexuality, homosexuality, transgender experience, cross dressing, poly sexual relationships, etc.) typically marginalized in contemporary American society. Write about what it would be like to be one of these characters managing marginalized sexual and/or gender identities or practices. Further, discuss what it was like to read a story where the majority of the characters occupy marginalized positions in contemporary American society.

3. Each of the characters in the novel manages something about themselves unknown to others. Pick a character, and discuss some reasons that character may or may not want others to know something about them. What might be some ways to fashion a social world wherein people would not feel the need to hide aspects of themselves?

4. Throughout the novel, we witness the ways the narrator experiences and makes sense of their own life as well as other people. Think about the ways you make sense of your own life and the others you encounter. What are some aspects of your experience others might not see on the surface, and what are some aspects of other people you may be unaware of when you interact with them?

5. Many characters in the novel go through changes as they age and encounter new terms, people, and experiences. Pick a character, and discuss some experiences or lessons that shaped that character's life and self concept. Do the same in relation to your own life.

6. Many characters reach and pass important milestones in the life course (i.e., first loves, first sexual encounters, finishing grade levels, changing schools, applying to college, etc.). Pick a character and discuss one of the major milestones they passed in the novel in relation to your own experience of that milestone or others you know who have passed that milestone.

7. The novel also explores some ways violence enters the lives of many Americans (i.e., accidents, suicides, conversion therapies, hate crimes and hate speech, etc.). While many Americans experience some or all of these aspects of our society, many other Americans do not experience any of them. Discuss the different ways these two groups of Americans might view violence in American society as well as American society as a whole.

8. *Cigarettes & Wine* takes place in the 1990s, and in the southeastern United States. Discuss the ways things may have changed and/or stayed the same in America, in the southeastern United States, and in the lives of varied LGBT and poly sexual people from different race, class, gender, sexual, religious, and regional backgrounds since then.

CREATIVE WRITING ASSIGNMENTS

1. Pick one of the main characters in the novel, and move forward in time ten years. What is their life like, where do they live, and what do they do for a living? Compose a story that answers these questions.

2. Re-write the first chapter of the novel from What's His Name's perspective.

3. Pick a character in the story, and write their story before, during, or after the events in the novel.

4. Beginning after the end of one of the last five chapters, write an alternative ending to the novel.

5. Pick a scene that the characters talk about in the book (i.e., some event you learn about in conversation, but do not witness with the narrator), and write that scene from the perspective of any character.

QUALITATIVE RESEARCH ACTIVITIES

1. Select any conversation or event in the book, and conduct a focus group to learn how other people interpret that conversation or event.
2. Select a character, and do a content analysis of that character. How do they talk? How do they see the world? What are their relationships (romantic, friendship, family, or otherwise) like? In what ways are they similar or different in relation to other characters? What information about them is missing and what information is presented in the novel? Overall, what can we learn from that character?

ABOUT THE AUTHOR

J. E. Sumerau, Ph.D., is an assistant professor of sociology and the director of applied sociology at the University of Tampa. Ze is also the co-founder of the academic blog Write Where It Hurts (www.writewhereithurts.net), and a regular contributor to the academic blogs Conditionally Accepted at Insider Higher Ed (https://www.insidehighered.com/users/conditionally-accepted) and The Society for the Study of Symbolic Interaction Music Blog (https://sssimusic.wordpress.com). Zir teaching, research, art and advocacy focuses on the intersections of sexualities, gender, religion, and health in the historical and interpersonal experiences of sexual, gender, and religious minorities, and has been published in numerous peer-reviewed academic journals and edited volumes. For more information, please visit www.jsumerau.com

CPSIA information can be obtained
at www.ICGtesting.com
Printed in the USA
LVOW13s0447090118
562341LV00002B/36/P